PERSON-CENTRED
COUNSELLING

Second Edition

Dave Mearns and
Brian Thorne

SAGE Publications
London • Thousand Oaks • New Delhi

First edition published 1988
Reprinted 1990, 1991, 1992, 1993, 1994, 1995, 1996, 1997
Second edition first published 1999. Reprinted 2000, 2001

 SAGE Publications Ltd
6 Bonhill Street
London EC2A 4PU

SAGE Publications Inc
2455 Teller Road
Thousand Oaks, California 91320

SAGE Publications India Pvt Ltd
32, M-Block Market
Greater Kailash – I
New Delhi 110 048

British Library Cataloguing in Publication Data

A catalogue record for this book is
available from the British Library

ISBN 0 7619 6316 2
ISBN 0 7619 63710 (pbk)

Library of Congress catalog record available

Typeset by M Rules
Printed and bound in Great Britain by Biddles Ltd,
www.biddles.co.uk

PERSON-CENTRED
COUNSELLING IN ACTION

Series Editor: Windy Dryden

SAGE's bestselling *Counselling in Action* series has gone from strength to strength, with worldwide sales of well over 250,000 copies. Since the first volumes in the series were published, the number of counselling courses has grown enormously, resulting in continuing demand for these introductory texts.

In response, and to keep pace with current developments in theory and practice, SAGE are pleased to announce that new and expanded editions of six of the volumes have now been published.

These short, practical books – developed especially for counsellors and students of counselling – will continue to provide clear and explicit guidelines for counselling practice.

New editions in the series include:

Feminist Counselling in Action, Second Edition
Jocelyn Chaplin
Cloth (0-7619-6310-3) / Paper (0-7619-6311-1)

Gestalt Counselling in Action, Second Edition
Petrūska Clarkson
Cloth (0-7619-6312-X) / Paper (0-7619-6313-8)

Transcultural Counselling in Action, Second Edition
Patricia d'Ardenne and Aruna Mahtani
Cloth (0-7619-6314-6) / Paper (0-7619-6315-4)

Rational Emotive Behavioural Counselling in Action, Second Edition
Windy Dryden
Cloth (0-7619-6302-2) / Paper (0-7619-6303-0)

Psychodynamic Counselling in Action, Second Edition
Michael Jacobs
Cloth (0-7619-6300-6) / Paper (0-7619-6301-4)

Person-Centred Counselling in Action, Second Edition
Dave Mearns and Brian Thorne
Cloth (0-7619-6316-2) / Paper (0-7619-6317-0)

This revised edition is dedicated to
Professor Windy Dryden whose indefatigable
energy and consummate editorial skill have
brought to fruition countless major contributions
to the professional literature of counselling
and psychotherapy.

CONTENTS

Acknowledgements

There are some people who have been particularly influential to us in our own development in relation to the person-centred approach, and we would like to take this opportunity to acknowledge their importance. An early influence for Dave Mearns was Ruth Pickford, who dared to introduce him to the unconventional psychologist Dr Carl Rogers, and a later and enduring Californian influence is Doug Land, who never 'teaches' but somehow helps people to learn what it means to be genuinely person-centred.

For Brian Thorne much is owed to Professor Bruce Shertzer, whose lecturing and supervision were a profound inspiration during basic training, and to Dr Chuck Devonshire, Founder of the Center for Cross-Cultural Communication and Co-founder of FDI (Britain), who has created many opportunities over the years for working with person-centred practitioners from many parts of the world.

While the first edition of this book was being written Carl Rogers, the originator of person-centred counselling, died shortly after his 85th birthday. The authors celebrate his life and work and this revised edition is an expression of their continuing desire to honour his memory and achievement.

PREFACE TO THE SECOND EDITION

The first edition of *Person-Centred Counselling in Action* was published in September 1988. The actual writing of the book had begun whilst Carl Rogers was still alive: indeed the writers hoped that he might be able to provide a foreword. His death on 5 February 1987 revealed something of a vacuum within the approach. There were thousands of practitioners world-wide and millions of other people who had been touched by person-centred practice and philosophy but, partly because Carl was such a prolific writer, there were scarcely any books on the discipline by other authors. With the centre of gravity for person-centred work moving from America to Europe, it was timely that two British authors should offer a fundamental book on the approach. The publication of *Person-Centred Counselling in Action* undoubtedly filled the vacuum. This fact, plus the ever-increasing popularity of the approach, resulted in high initial sales of the book and the unusual statistical record of sales having increased in each of its eleven years of publication. In 1996, *Person-Centred Counselling in Action* became the bestselling book of all time and across all academic disciplines, published by Sage (U.K.) Ltd.

Person-Centred Counselling in Action was not only the most widely read book in the popular 'Counselling in Action' series edited by Windy Dryden, but it also heralded a series of person-centred books published by Sage (U.K.). In 1992 Brian Thorne produced *Carl Rogers*, a critical study which has been widely acclaimed throughout the world. *Developing Person-Centred Counselling* was written by Dave Mearns in 1994. The objective of this book was to introduce developments in the approach presented concisely in 30 short sections. This presented a mixture of old and new ideas to challenge the more experienced practitioner. The first major text ever written on the pedagogy of person-centred counselling was published as *Person-Centred Counselling Training* in 1997, again by Dave Mearns. By this time the pace of publishing was hotting up and in 1998 we had three prominent Sage (U.K.) offerings with David Rennie's *Person-Centred Counselling: An Experiential Approach;* Brian Thorne and Elke Lambers's *Person-Centred Therapy: A European Perspective*; and Goff Barrett-Lennard's *Carl Rogers' Helping System: Journey & Substance.*

This last book, comprising more than 400 pages, represents 20 years' work on the part of Goff Barrett-Lennard and offers a text which not only analyses the approach but documents its many pathways throughout the world over 50 years. Also this year (1999) Sage publishes Charlie O'Leary's*Counselling Couples and Famies: A Person-Centred Approach*, the first book ever produced exploring the person-centred view of relationship therapy. These books have not been part of a planned series but each has won publication on its own merit and together they not only represent the development of the approach but also illustrate the central role played by Sage (U.K.) in publishing within the person-centred tradition.

Since writing the first edition of *Person-Centred Counselling in Action* in 1988 the authors have deepened their involvement with the approach. **Dave Mearns** has published another four books and numerous academic articles delving more deeply not only into the practice of person-centred counselling but also into the Self theory which underpins it. He has been fascinated by the fact that even in such an apparently 'open' relationship as counselling, there is still a large 'unspoken relationship' between client and counsellor. If that can be 'tapped' respectfully, then there are considerable possibilities for learning – both for the client but also for the counsellor! (Mearns, 1994) Dave has also been trying to put the therapeutic conditions back together again with his integrative notion of 'working at relational depth' (Mearns, 1996, 1997a). The therapeutic conditions were separated for ease of definition, research and training but the defining feature of skilful practice in the person-centred counsellor is their coherent integration. In recent times Dave has begun to explore and further develop the theory of 'Self' upon which Carl Rogers based the approach. In this work, which will be published during 1999 and 2000, a look is taken inside the Self of the client to find the various 'configurations' which interrelate to create the functioning unit. Interestingly, many of the dynamics we find within the Self mirror those of person-centred family therapy described by Charlie O'Leary.

Brian Thorne's interests have taken him in a somewhat different direction although he, too, has increasingly demonstrated the power of the approach when working in depth with clients. He has provided convincing evidence to refute the common criticism that person-centred counselling is effective only in the relief of comparatively superficial concerns expressed by the middle-classes. As a practising Christian who has made significant contributions in the field of pastoral theology (e.g. Thorne, 1991b), Brian has focused on the later work of Carl Rogers and, together with prominent European colleagues, he has explored the implications for both theory and practice of the openness to spiritual experience of the approach. In two major collections of papers, *Person-centred Counselling: Therapeutic and Spiritual Dimensions* (1991a) and *Person-centred Counselling and Christian Spirituality* (1998), both published by Whurr Publishers of London, he has not only demonstrated the power of the approach in enabling clients to face the deepest existential questions but has also shown the profound interconnectedness of spirituality and sexuality. Currently Brian is preoccupied with professional and political questions as counselling and psychotherapy come to occupy a more prominent position in European society. He is involved in fundamental debates about the compatibility of person-centred theory and practice with the increasingly prescriptive frameworks which are emerging for registration and accreditation (Thorne, 1997a; 1997b).

In creating this second edition of *Person-Centred Counselling in Action*, we have included reference to the work since 1988 but we have not sought to incorporate this in detail. Instead, we have tried to maintain the shape and the level of the book while updating its content in the light of experience. Approximately 5,000 words have been added to the first edition and very little has been taken out. Most chapters have had additions and revisions although very few changes have been made to the case study presentation which constitutes Chapters 6, 7 and 8. After reflection, we felt we could not improve on this case study not only in terms of the variety of points it raises but also in the collaborative exercise it represents between counsellor and client.

In the second edition we have not changed our 'position' on any of the theoretical or practical issues, although at times we have sought to point out the effect of changing circumstances over these past 11 years. We have, however, improved upon our frequent use of the term 'organismic self', mainly in Chapter 1 of the first edition. While this was rather a neat, concise conceptualisation of tendencies which were basic to human functioning, it was confusing for students to regard such tendencies as constituting a 'Self'. Just to prove that teachers sometimes do learn from their students, we began to question the use of this term ourselves and researched it historically. Interestingly, while we found that the term was employed by a number of person-centred writers, we could not trace any references to its use by Carl Rogers himself. Carl wrote about fundamental tendencies such as the *'actualising tendency'* and the *'organismic valuing process'* but he did not constitute these in the form of any kind of basic 'Self'. We have rewritten some of Chapter 1 to make the language more consistent with that of the theory. This should create less confusion in the minds of new readers. Incidentally, there is an international prize on offer to the first student or academic who can give a line reference to Carl Rogers using the term *'organismic self'* in any published work. Prospective claimants should contact Dave Mearns directly!

We are excited about producing this second edition of *Person-Centred Counselling in Action* before the end of the millennium. It has been a great pleasure for us to re-live the experience of cooperative writing in the shaping of this new edition. We hope that the outcome of our labours also proves interesting and pleasurable to the reader.

Professor David Mearns,
University of Strathclyde,
Glasgow

Professor Brian Thorne
University of East Anglia
Norwich

Introduction

Person-centred counselling has its origins in the pioneering work in the 1930s and 1940s of Dr Carl Rogers, the American psychologist and therapist. During this period Rogers was gradually developing his own style of therapy, which he saw as a radical departure from the analytical approach. The central truth for Rogers was that the client knows best. It is the client who knows what is hurting and in the final analysis it is the client who knows how to move forward. So convinced was Rogers of this fundamental insight that he first called his way of working 'non-directive' counselling, thereby emphasising that the counsellor's task is to enable the client to make contact with his own inner resources rather than to guide, advise or in some other way influence the direction the client should take. Later on Rogers became somewhat exasperated with those ill-informed critics who took pleasure in depicting him and his associates as passive nodders wedded to a policy of inactivity, and he began to describe his work as 'client-centred' counselling, thus emphasising the central importance of the client's phenomenological world. Many practitioners throughout the world continue to define themselves in this way and this book might well have been entitled 'Client-Centred Counselling in Action'.

We have opted for the expression 'person-centred counselling' in recognition of the fact that what began as a distinctive approach to counselling has in the past 30 or so years extended its influence into many other fields including education, management, cross-cultural communication and international peace work. Rogers coined the term the 'person-centred

1

approach' in order to do justice to this remarkable extension of his work, and as a way of describing a set of values, attitudes and behaviours when they were being employed in contexts far removed from the traditional one-to-one setting of a therapeutic interview. So widespread is this term now that journals for practitioners and researchers are entitled *The Person-Centered Journal* and *Person-Centred Practice*.

Our choice of title was prompted by a further consideration which deserves elaboration. It seems to us that the counselling relationships in which we engage require of us the utmost concentration on, and aware-ness of, our own thoughts, feelings, sensations and intuitions in the moment-to-moment interaction with our clients. If the truth be known we are not merely focused on the world of our clients. We are concerned to be in touch with ourselves as much as with them, and to monitor ceaselessly the relationship between us. Person-centred counselling therefore seems a thoroughly apt description of our work, for we are at all times in this highly concentrated way committed as persons to other persons who seek our help.

It should not be imagined, that by opting for the term 'person-centred counselling' we are in any sense abandoning the discipline and rigour which characterised the first flourishing of client-centred counselling in America, when Rogers and his associates were widely acknowledged as in the vanguard of both practice and research. On the contrary, we are pleading for a return to such discipline, and are little short of horrified by the continuing proliferation of counselling practitioners, both in America and in Britain, who seem to believe that by sticking the label person-cen-tred on themselves they have licence to follow the most bizarre promptings of their own intuition or to create a veritable smorgasbord of therapeutic approaches which smack of eclecticism at its most irresponsible. Person-centred counselling as we practise it is 'traditional' in its emphasis on the full involvement of the counsellor in the relationship with the client. To us that 'old' foundation presents new challenges every day of our working lives.

In Britain, where the authors of this book are based, the person-centred approach has received considerable stimulus in the past 15 years from the development of a number of specialised training courses, distin-guished by the *depth* of their working in the approach. Previously, there was a tendency for the approach to be taught by people who had not themselves been trained in depth, the result of which was that person-cen-tred counselling became viewed as 'superficial'.

This book is designed to focus primarily on counselling *practice* rather than theory; hence, while there is a wealth of practical illustrations and excerpts from cases, there is a relative dearth of research analysis. One consequence of this is that the work of eminent American person-centred practitioner/researchers is under-represented. The development of the person-centred approach cannot be fully understood without reference to this work by, amongst others, Fred Zimring, John Shlien, Julius Seeman, Nat Raskin, Cecil Patterson, Eugene Gendlin, Art Combs, Jerry Bozarth, David Cain and Garry Prouty. This book also substantially neglects work of major European researchers, such as Reinhard Tausch of Germany and Germain Lietaer of Belgium. Fortunately, the recent book by Goff Barrett-Lennard (1998), also by Sage Publications, gives a comprehensive account of the development of the approach and its embeddedness in theory and research.

Person-Centred Counselling in Action is written in such a way that it will be relevant to practitioners, students and clients in America, Europe and most other parts of the world, but there are two points of cross-cultural difference which should be clarified. Firstly, there are many references to the work which the counsellor does with her *supervisor*. This emphasis on supervision reflects the counselling setting in Britain where continued accreditation as a counsellor with the British Association for Counselling (BAC) requires life-long supervision, a condition which is not obligatory in most parts of America and Europe.

A second point for clarification centres on the use of the words *counselling* and *psychotherapy*. Within the person-centred approach these two terms are not usually distinguished because the *processes* involved between practitioner and client remain the same whether we call the activity 'psychotherapy' or 'counselling'. The situation is further complicated by the fact that in Britain the word *counselling* tends to be used in contexts which in America might warrant the term *psychotherapy*. In the opening chapter of an influential book, Patterson (1974) presents an informative analysis of the problem of distinguishing between counselling and psychotherapy, but in this book we have stayed consistent to the policy of the series by referring to our work as 'counselling' and by confining ourselves to relatively short-term therapeutic relationships. None of the cases presented in this book continued for the one or two years which some workers would regard as a criterion for labelling the activity 'psychotherapy'.

The last issue we wish to address in this introduction is our choice of personal pronouns throughout the book. Many books on counselling use both *he* and *she*, but there is a tendency for most counsellors to be male while clients are largely female! In our British experience, however, female counsellors clearly outnumber their male counterparts; hence our general usage makes the counsellor female and, for the sake of clarity, the client is usually male. There are exceptions where this convention is reversed, especially when case material would otherwise be falsified or its force reduced. Of one thing we are absolutely sure: men and women are all unique persons and any literary convention which appears to demean them individuals or as members of their sex is to be rejected.

The book's structure reflects our primary aim of enabling the reader to enter into the living experience of person-centred counselling. This is a book for practitioners or would-be practitioners and for their clients. The opening chapter attempts to explore the major theoretical constructs which underpin the approach both in terms of personality development and therapeutic process, but thereafter each chapter is concerned to illustrate in as concrete a way as possible the attitudes, skills, dilemmas and moment-to-moment challenges of the person-centred counsellor at work. The final three chapters draw extensively on the experience of one particular therapeutic relationship and we are much indebted to the client, Joan, for her willingness to be fully participant in the process of reflecting on her therapeutic journey and for her cooperation in monitoring the form of its presentation in this book. We hope that the reader, too, will be encouraged to reflect on his or her own therapeutic journey whether as counsellor or client, and will share with us something of the excitement of attempting to capture in words the beauty and mystery of the person-to-person encounter which we call counselling.

THE PERSON-CENTRED APPROACH

THEORIES, EXPERTS AND EFFICIENCY

In some academic quarters the person-centred approach to counselling receives scant attention. There are at least two powerful reasons for this. In the first place the approach lays primary stress on the quality of the relationship between counsellor and client. Secondly, it is not concerned to impose a plethora of externally derived theory upon the experiencing of the client – instead, the aim is to help the client to unravel the 'personal theory' which he has constructed around his own experiencing. There are some intellectuals, however, who delight in theoretical complexity and also tend to be somewhat apprehensive about relationships which seem to demand too deep an involvement. It is therefore not surprising that both in academic and professional circles the person-centred approach can sometimes be dismissed as facile or superficial, or even castigated as naive or misguidedly optimistic. Another common or patronising response is to regard person-centred counselling as simply embodying what all good counsellors do anyway at the beginning of a therapeutic relationship – before, that is, they pass on to deploy much more sophisticated techniques which can *really* deal with the client's problems.

There can be little doubt that in many ways the person-centred approach is strikingly out of alignment with much that characterises the current culture of the western world. The late Carl Rogers, its originator and its most eminent practitioner, often commented that his way of being and working ran counter to the mechanistic ethos of a technological society which thrives on efficiency, quick answers and the role of expert. In Rogers' view such an ethos has the effect of reducing human beings to the level of objects and of placing disproportionate power in the hands of a few. What is more, it gives ample scope to those who seem only too willing to hand over responsibility for their lives to others, whether out of fear or because of apathy. The person-centred point of view, however, places high value on the experience of the individual human being and on the importance of his or her subjective reality. It also challenges each person to accept responsibility for his or her own life and to trust in the inner resources which are available to all those who are prepared to set out along the path of self-awareness and self-acceptance.

THE SELF-CONCEPT

The distrust of experts runs deep among person-centred practitioners. In some ways it is fair to state that the person-centred counsellor must learn to wear her expertise as an invisible garment if she is to become an effective counsellor. Experts are expected to dispense their expertise, to recommend what should be done, to offer authoritative guidance or even to issue orders. Clearly there are some areas of human experience where such expertise is essential and appropriate. Unfortunately all too many of those who seek the help of counsellors have spent much of their lives surrounded by people who, with devastating inappropriateness, have appointed themselves experts in the conduct of other people's lives. As a result such clients are in despair at their inability to fulfil the expectations of others, whether parents, teachers, colleagues or so-called friends, and have no sense of self-respect or personal worth. And yet, despite the damage they have already suffered at the hands of those who have tried to direct their lives for them, such people will often come to a counsellor searching for yet another expert to tell them what to do. Person-centred counsellors, while accepting and understanding this desperate need for external authority, will do all they can to avoid falling into the trap of fulfilling such a role. To do so would be to deny a central assumption of the approach, namely that the client can be trusted to find his own way forward if only the counsellor can be the kind of companion who is capable of encouraging a relationship where the client can begin, however tentatively, to feel safe and to experience the first intimations of self-acceptance. The odds against this happening are sometimes formidable because the view the client has of himself is low and the judgemental 'experts' in his life, both past and present, have been so powerfully destructive. The gradual revelation of a client's *self-concept*, that is the person's conceptual construction of himself (however poorly expressed), can be harrowing in the extreme for the listener. The full extent of an individual's self-rejection often proves a stern challenge to the counsellor's faith, both in the client and in her own capacity to become a reliable companion in the therapeutic process.

The brief extract in Box 1.1 captures the sad and almost inexorable development of a self-concept which then undermines everything that a person does or tries to be. There is a sense of worthlessness and of being doomed to rejection and disapproval. Once such a self-concept has been internalised the person tends to reinforce it, for it is a fundamental tenet of the person-centred viewpoint that our behaviour is to a large extent an acting-out of the way we actually feel about ourselves and the world we inhabit. In essence what we do is often a reflection of how we evaluate ourselves and if we have come to the conclusion that we are inept, worthless and unacceptable it is more than likely that we shall behave in a way which demonstrates the validity of such an assessment. The chances, therefore, of winning esteem or approval become more and more remote as time goes on.

Box 1.1 The Evolution of the Poor Self-Concept

CLIENT: I don't remember my parents ever praising me for anything. They always had something critical to say. My mother was always on about my untidiness, my lack of thought about everything. My father was always calling me stupid. When I got six 'A' passes in my GCSEs he said it was typical that I had done well in the wrong subjects.

COUNSELLOR: It seems you could never do anything right in their eyes no matter how hard you tried or how successful you were.

CLIENT: My friends were just as bad. They kept on at me about my appearance and told me that I was a pimply swot. I just wanted to creep around without being seen by anyone.

COUNSELLOR: You felt so awful about yourself that you would like to have been invisible.

CLIENT: It's not all in the past. It's just the same now. My husband never approves of anything I do and now my daughter says she's ashamed to bring her friends home in case I upset them. It seems I'm no use to anyone. It would be better if I just disappeared.

CONDITIONS OF WORTH

Fortunately the disapproval and rejection which many people experience is not such as to be totally annihilating. They are left with at least some shreds of self-esteem although these may often feel so fragile that the fear of final condemnation is never far away. It is as if such people are living according to a kind of legal contract, and that they only have to put one foot wrong for the whole weight of the law to descend upon them. They struggle, therefore, to keep themselves afloat by trying to do and to be those things which they know will elicit approval while scrupulously avoiding or suppressing those thoughts, feelings and activities which they sense will bring adverse judgement. Their sense of worth, both in their own eyes and in those of others who have been important to them, is conditional upon winning approval and avoiding disapproval, and this means that their range of behaviour is severely restricted for they can only behave in ways which are sure to be acceptable to others. They are the victims of the '*conditions of worth*' which others have imposed upon them, but so great is their need for positive approval that they accept this straitjacket rather than risk rejection by trespassing against the conditions set for their acceptability.

Sometimes, though, the situation is such that they can no longer play this contractual game and then their worst fears may be realised as they experience the disapproval and the growing rejection of the other person (see Box 1.2).

Box 1.2 Conditions of Worth

CLIENT: Everything was all right at first. I knew that he admired my bright conversation and the way I dressed. He liked the way I made love to him, too. I used to make a point of chatting when he came in and of making sure that I was well turned out even after a busy day at the office.

COUNSELLOR: You knew how to win his approval and you were happy to fulfil the necessary conditions.

CLIENT: Yes, but that all changed when I got pregnant. I wanted to talk about the baby but he wasn't interested it seemed. He obviously didn't like what was happening to my figure and I used to feel so tired that I hadn't the energy for the sort of love-making he wanted. He got more and more moody and I felt more and more depressed.

COUNSELLOR: You were no longer acceptable to him or to yourself.

THE ORGANISMIC VALUING PROCESS

A poor self concept and countless internalised conditions of worth are typical attributes of clients coming for counselling. Such people are cut off from their essential resources as human beings and divorced from their intrinsic ability to make judgements about their existence – their *organismic valuing process* in Rogers' terminology. The human organism, it is argued, can essentially be relied upon to provide the individual with trustworthy messages, and this is discernible in the physiological processes of the entire body and through the process of growth by which an individual's potentialities and capacities are brought to realisation. This fundamental, intrinsic or 'organismic' valuing process helps the person to have a sense of what they need for their enhancement both from their environment and from other people. Unfortunately, however, the need for the positive regard and approval of others is overwhelming, and not infrequently this need takes precedence over the promptings of the intrinsic valuing process which, if followed, could perhaps earn the anger or displeasure of a parent or other significant person whose approval is crucial to the individual's physical and psychological well-being. When the organismic valuing process comes into conflict with the need for approval the outcome must be confusion (see Box 1.3), and where this happens repeatedly a person will be forced to develop a self-concept which serves to estrange him almost completely from his organismic experiencing or to make him profoundly distrustful of it.

Box 1.3 Early Confusion of the Organismic Valuing Process

CHILD: [*Falls over and cuts his knee: runs crying to his mother for comfort or assurance.*]

MOTHER: What a silly thing to do. Stop crying and do not be such a baby. It's hardly bleeding.

CHILD: [*Thinks: it's stupid to fall over; it's wrong to cry; I shouldn't want mummy's support but I need it. But I wanted to cry; I wanted mummy's cuddle: I wasn't stupid. I don't know what to do. Who can I trust? I need mummy's love but I want to cry.*]

The loss of trust in the promptings of the organismic valuing process can result in the creation of a self-concept which attempts to blot out such promptings altogether, or to view them with the most critical scepticism. A person who has been told repeatedly, for example, that it is wrong and destructive to be angry may arrive at the point where he says of himself, 'I am a person who never feels angry', or, just as disastrously, 'I am a person who deserves punishment because I am always feeling angry.' In the first case the promptings of anger have been totally repressed from consciousness, whereas in the second they are a cause for self-condemnation and guilt. In both cases the resulting self-concept is far removed from any sense of trust in the reliability of the organismic valuing of direct and untrammelled experience. In counselling there sometimes comes a crucial moment when trust in the dependability of the organismic valuing process is restored, however temporary or partial this may be (see Box 1.4). Such moments do much to strengthen the counsellor's faith in the client's ability to find his own way forward and point to the *actualising tendency* or innate capacity in all human beings to move towards the fulfilment of their potential. At the deepest level there is in all of us a yearning and the wherewithal to become more than we are.

Box 1.4 The Organismic Valuing Process is Restored

CLIENT: I feel very sad: it's an overwhelming feeling.

COUNSELLOR: As if you have no option but to give yourself to the sadness.

CLIENT: That sounds very frightening – as if I shall lose control. But I never lose control. [*Suddenly bursts into tears.*]

COUNSELLOR: Your tears speak for you.

CLIENT: But big boys don't cry.

COUNSELLOR: Are you saying that you are ashamed of your tears?

CLIENT: [*Long pause.*] No . . . for the first time for years I feel in touch with myself . . . It feels OK to be crying.

THE LOCUS OF EVALUATION

The person who has been unlucky enough to be surrounded by those who are sharply critical and judgemental will have been forced to resort to all manner of strategies in order to achieve a modicum of approval and positive regard. In almost all cases this will have entailed a progressive alienation from the organismic valuing process and the creation of a self-concept which is divorced from the person's innate resources and wisdom. The self-concept is likely to be poor but in some cases the person establishes a picture of himself which enables him to retain a degree of self-respect through a total blocking off from all significant sensory or 'visceral' experience. In all such cases, however, the organismic valuing process has ceased in any significant way to be a source of knowledge or guidance for the individual. He is likely to have great difficulty in making decisions or in knowing what he thinks or feels. There will probably be a reliance on external authorities for guidance or a desperate attempt to please everyone which often results in unpredictable, inconsistent and incongruent behaviour.

Psychologically healthy persons are men and women who have been fortunate enough to be surrounded by others whose acceptance and approval have enabled them to develop self-concepts which allow them for at least some of the time to be in touch with their deepest feelings and experiences. They are not cut off from the ground of their being and they are well placed to move towards becoming what Rogers has described as 'fully functioning' persons (Rogers, 1963). Such people are open to experience without feeling threatened and are consequently able to listen to themselves and to others. They are highly aware of their feelings and the feelings of others and they have the capacity to live in the present moment. Most importantly, they display a trust and confidence in their organismic valuing process which is manifestly lacking in those who have continually had to battle with the adverse judgement of others. Such trusting is most evident in the process of decision-making and in the awareness and articulation of present thoughts and feelings. Instead of searching for guidance from outside or experiencing an internal confusion or blankness, the fully functioning person has his or her source of wisdom deep within and accessible. Rogers has described this self-referent as the internal *locus of evaluation* and for the counsellor one of the most significant moments in therapy is the point when a client recognises this reference point within himself perhaps for the first time (Box 1.5).

Box 1.5 The Internal Locus of Evaluation

CLIENT: I suppose I went into the job to please my father. It seemed to make sense, too, in terms of having some sort of career structure.

COUNSELLOR: It was important to please your father and to feel OK in conventional career terms.

CLIENT: Yes – and I have a feeling I married Jean because I knew my parents liked her. I certainly wasn't in love with her.

COUNSELLOR: You married her to please them, really.

CLIENT: And last night I knew that I can't go on. I hate the job and my marriage is a farce. I've got to find out what I want, what makes sense to me, before I waste the whole of my life trying to please other people. And I think I'm beginning to get some glimmering of what I must do. It's very frightening to hear your own voice for the first time.

THE CREATION AND CONTINUATION OF DISTURBANCE

The person-centred counsellor is alert to understanding the self-concept of her client and will rapidly discover that in most instances the evolution of that self-concept has been profoundly affected by the adverse judgement of others. It has also involved an increasingly ambivalent attitude on the individual's part towards his ability to evaluate his own experience. In short, thanks to the condemnation and criticism of others, the person has grown more and more doubtful of the validity and the acceptability of his own thoughts and feelings. He needs approval and affirmation, but the only way of obtaining these has been to deny the appropriateness and the rightness of the promptings of his valuing process. Instead, in many cases the only possible strategy has involved the almost total rejection of its validity and the substitution of a code of behaviour around which a self-concept has been fashioned. This self-concept, far from representing the confident evaluation of his own experience reflects instead other people's prejudices. It will contain many imperatives such as 'I *should* behave this way', 'I *ought* to feel that way', 'I am the kind of person who must always be kind/considerate/hard/aggressive'. Once this process is well under way the person can be said to be disturbed in the sense that self-experience and the self-concept are to a marked degree in conflict. Unfortunately the likelihood is that this disturbance will be maintained and even intensified as the individual seeks to preserve and consolidate the self-concept in order to bolster his own sense of security or to avoid criticism and rejection. Once this process has become a way of life the chances are that the person will no longer be capable of hearing the whisperings of his organismic valuing process at all and will certainly have lost any sense of an inner resourcefulness for making decisions and taking action. Such a person is likely to be unhappy and to have a poor self-concept, however much this is concealed from others (highly 'successful' people sometimes feel that they are impostors). There are also examples of self-assured and confident individuals who are nonetheless seriously disturbed because they have long since lost their intrinsic sense of who they are and have successfully put in place a self-concept whose authenticity they themselves no longer question and with which they feel satisfied or even smug. Such people are unlikely to cross the counsellor's threshold unless a traumatic episode suddenly brings the whole edifice of the carefully constructed self-concept tumbling down (see Box 1.6).

Box 1.6 When Crisis Strikes the Edifice Can Collapse

John had lived his life detached from his organismic valuing process. Cathy, his wife, had frequently bemoaned his 'lack of *real* feelings', but she has only recently broken their relationship. This has hit John like a thunderbolt, for he never imagined it could happen. It has shaken his ill-founded self-concept to its core. His feelings, buried for years past, have now been tumbling out whenever he talks to anyone. For the first time he mourns his child who died 15 years ago. He cries for everything – most particularly for his loss of an intrinsic sense of his own identity.

It follows from the person-centred view of psychological disturbance that such disturbance will be continued and reinforced if an individual remains dependent to a large extent on the positive judgement of others for a sense of self-worth. Such a person will expend much energy on defending the self-concept which wins the approval and esteem of others. If it is threatened there will be fear and confusion. The self-assured individual referred to above is likely in such circumstances to resort to one or other of two basic mechanisms of defence: perceptual distortion or denial. If an episode of traumatic intensity occurs then such defences are likely to prove inadequate, but often enough they will serve to preserve the current self-concept. The self-assured man, for example, might allow himself to experience another person's criticism of him, but would distort this as unjustifiable intrusion on the part of someone whom he labels in his own eyes as an interfering busy-body. Denial is a less common defence but when it occurs it is the more impregnable. In this case the individual preserves his self-concept by completely evading any conscious contact with experiences or feelings which threaten him. The self-assured man would therefore be totally unaware of his dominating arrogance, for example, and might well see this as simply forceful expression of his insightful analysis of a situation. He would in consequence be impervious to the distress or resentment of his colleagues, and if he vaguely sensed their hostility he might well see no connection between this and his own behaviour.

It will be evident that the person-centred counsellor has an optimistic perspective on the inherent potential of the human being. This is not the same as suggesting that we are by definition born pure and without defect, a kind of virtuous tabula rasa, but it is undoubtedly a point of view which runs counter to many of the pessimistic beliefs enshrined in certain religious and psychological systems. The person-centred counsellor believes that each individual has the potential to become a unique and beautiful creation, but that none of us can do this alone and unaided. Unfortunately, as the life history of so many clients shows, other people can provide not the nourishment for growth but the poison which can weaken and even destroy the human spirit. In this sense Sartre is right when he describes hell as other people – and yet ironically, these other people also have the potential to become fully functioning individuals. It seems that so often we do not know how to live with each other in such a way that we can grow and flourish together. This is the distressing reality which many counselling clients know only too well and which the person-centred counsellor acknowledges but refuses to accept as the final answer.

CREATING THE CONDITIONS FOR GROWTH

The person-centred counsellor believes that all clients have within themselves vast resources for development. They have the capacity to grow towards the fulfilment of their unique identities, which means that self-concepts are not unalterable and attitudes or behaviours can be modified or transformed. Where development is blocked or distorted this is the outcome of relationships which have trampled upon the individual's innate and basic need for positive regard, and which have led to the creation of a self-concept and accompanying behaviour that serve as a defence against attack and disapproval. The counsellor's task is to create new conditions of relationship where the growth process can be encouraged and the stunting or warping remedied. In a sense the counsellor attempts to provide different soil and a different climate in which the client can recover from past deprivation or maltreatment and begin to flourish as the unique individual he or she actually is. It is the nature of this new relationship environment and the counsellor's ability to create it that are central to the whole therapeutic enterprise.

It is possible to describe the nature of the growth-producing climate briefly and clearly. Rogers believed that it is characterised by three conditions. The first element focuses on the realness, or genuineness, or *congruence* of the counsellor. The more the counsellor is able to be herself in the relationship without putting up a professional front or a personal façade the greater will be the chance of the client changing and developing in a positive and constructive manner. The counsellor who is congruent conveys the message that it is not only permissible but desirable to be oneself. She also presents herself as transparent to the client and thus refuses to encourage an image of herself as superior, expert, omniscient. In such a relationship the client is more likely to find resources within himself and will not cling to the expectations that the counsellor will provide the answers for him. The second requirement in creating a climate for change and growth is the counsellor's ability to offer the client a total acceptance, a cherishing, an *unconditional positive regard*. When the counsellor is able to embrace this attitude of acceptance and non-judgementalism then therapeutic movement is much more likely. The client is more able to feel safe to explore negative feelings and to move into the core of his anxiety or depression. He is also more likely to face himself honestly without the ever-present fear of rejection or condemnation. What is more the intensive experience of the counsellor's acceptance is the context in which he is most likely to sense the first momentary feelings of self-acceptance. The third element which is necessary in the therapeutic relationship is *empathic understanding*. When this is present the counsellor demonstrates a capacity to track and sense accurately the feelings and personal meanings of the client; she is able to learn what it feels like to be in the client's skin and to perceive the world as the client perceives it. What is more, she develops the ability to communicate to the client this sensitive and acceptant understanding. To be understood in this way is for many

clients a rare or even an unique experience. It indicates to them a preparedness on the part of the counsellor to offer attention and a level of
caring which undeniably endows them with value. Furthermore when a
person is deeply understood in this way it is difficult to maintain for long
a stance of alienation and separation. Empathic understanding restores to
the lonely and alienated individual a sense of belonging to the human
race. These three elements in the therapeutic relationship are summarised
in Box 1.7. They are often referred to in the person-centred literature as
the *core conditions* and were constantly reiterated by Rogers (Rogers, 1951,
1961, 1974, 1979, 1980a).

Box 1.7 The Core Conditions

The creation of a growth-producing climate in a therapeutic relationship
requires that the counsellor can:

1 be genuine or congruent
2 offer unconditional positive regard and total acceptance
3 feel and communicate a deep empathic understanding.

The core conditions are simple enough to state, but for a counsellor to
develop and maintain such attitudes involves a lifetime's work and
demands a commitment which has profound implications not only for the
counsellor's professional activity but for her life as a whole. Much of this
book, indeed, is devoted to an exploration of the complex issues involved
when a counsellor attempts to be congruent, accepting and empathic.
The words can trip off the tongue but their significance is little short of
awe-inspiring.

ADDITIONAL BELIEFS OF THE PERSON-CENTRED COUNSELLOR

It is tempting to stop with this clear exposition of the person-centred
approach and, in a sense, all that is most important has been said once
attention has been focused on the hypothesis of the inherent growth principle and on the theory of the core conditions for therapeutic movement.
   In an interesting paper, however, Bozarth and Temaner Brodley (1986)

have attempted to explore what they see as a number of supporting assertions which follow from Rogers' central propositions and which are likely
therefore to feature in the underlying belief system of the person-centred
counsellor. These assertions throw an illuminating light on both the
theory and the practice of person-centred counselling.

The first series of assertions which Bozarth and Temaner Brodley
advance is concerned with the essential nature of human beings. The
belief that all human beings have within them the innate capacity to grow
towards their own unique fulfilment, spurred on by the actualising tendency, is buttressed by four further propositions. Human nature, it is
postulated, is *essentially constructive* and not destructive. It is indeed this
belief which frequently draws the criticism that the person-centred
approach is over-optimistic or naive and does less than justice to the
'shadow' or 'dark' side of the human psyche. The person-centred counsellor, however, sees destructive behaviour and feelings as simply
manifestations of the person who is by nature essentially constructive
and self-preserving when that person is functioning under unfavourable
conditions. Aggression and destructiveness are interpreted as resources
which the person brings into play when his desire to grow is thwarted or
threatened or when, in potentially terrible circumstances, his very existence is at stake. Secondly, human nature is seen as *basically social* so
that human beings are by nature protective, caring, compassionate and
understanding towards each other. It is argued that the dependence of
human infants and the interdependence of adults points in this direction,
as does the innate capacity to infer imaginatively the experience of others.
The third proposition asserts that *self-regard* is a *basic human need* and
this is linked to an extreme position of respect for persons so that every
effort is made by person-centred practitioners not to violate a person's
sense of autonomy, resourcefulness and self-respect. The final proposition
in this first series of supporting assertions is that *human beings are basically motivated to pursue the truth*; that they have, in effect, a scientific
nature which wants to tease out the reality of situations and does not wish
to seek refuge in deception or half-truth.

The second series of assertions presented by Bozarth and Temaner
Brodley is more concerned with the beliefs which influence directly the
counsellor's behaviour and attitude towards her clients. The first is a kind
of rationale for the importance of empathy. It follows from the 'scientific'
nature of human beings that what a person perceives is a major determi-
nant of personal experience and of behaviour. Logically, therefore, it is
clear that *to understand a person one must attempt to grasp his or her way*

of perceiving reality or, in short, one must understand empathically. The second assertion underscores the person-centred counsellor's *commitment to the individual* as at all times *the primary reference point*, even if the context is the facilitation of a group or the fostering of improvement in a family or an organisation. So-called 'group realities' are therefore treated with scepticism, and what may be regarded as extreme measures are taken to ensure that individuals are not sacrificed on the altar of group goals. The third assertion commits the person-centred counsellor to a belief in the *concept of the whole person.* Such a belief will enable the counsellor to avoid the danger of relating only to a fragment of her client and her client's experience. It will underline, too, the awareness that people grow and change and continually discover and reveal more of themselves. Such a belief will enable the counsellor to be patient and tolerant, and even hopeful in the face of despair. It will also lead to moments of joy and awe when further facets of the unique person are revealed. It emphasises, too, that to relate to a person in the present means by definition relating to his past and his future. The fourth assertion in this second series proposes that *persons are trying their best to grow and to protect themselves* in the light of the internal and external circumstances that exist at that time. In short, the counsellor is invited to trust the client's real desire to do the best he can, even if the resulting behaviour is felt to be from some perspectives bad, wrong or misguided (see example in Box 1.8). Persons are not totally in control of themselves nor totally self-determining. They do what they

---

Box 1.8 People Do the Best They Can, in Their Circumstances

Bob was neither a popular boss nor an easy partner. As a boss he was brusque, task-centred, technically efficient and disregarding of others. As a partner he was the same. He had developed a way of being which kept him safe and uninvolved within human relationships. The metaphor he used for his life was that he travelled on a smooth and powerful ocean liner, but he travelled alone.

Much earlier in life Bob had found his way to survive conditions of worth which punished him for the slightest 'weakness' and which rewarded him only with cold 'approval'. In any circumstances the *actualising tendency* pushes us to do the best we can to maintain and enhance our functioning. But Bob had to achieve this while avoiding what others might call 'weakness'. Bob had done a remarkable job.

---

can and it is therefore appropriate neither to blame nor to give excessive merit to people for their actions. This does not mean that we are not responsible for what we do. We remain responsible even when we cannot help our actions and we exercise responsibility by pursuing self-awareness as the means of effecting change both within ourselves and within our circumstances.

The final assertion offered by Bozarth and Temaner Brodley is of such central importance to the whole practice of person-centred counselling that it requires separate discussion. Its implications, furthermore, go far beyond the therapeutic arena and extend into almost all domains of social and political life. They point to the person-centred counsellor's belief in the *importance of rejecting the pursuit of control or authority* over other persons. Alongside this there is the corresponding commitment to share power and to exercise control co-operatively. In the counselling relationship this implies an ever-watchful attentiveness to any imbalance between counsellor and client and a constant seeking to equalise power through any procedures, whether verbal or otherwise, which can remedy such imbalance. This emphasis on the abdication from power-seeking reinforces even more vigorously the person-centred value that authority about the client lies in the client and not in an outside expert. Bozarth and Temaner Brodley mention with much justification that this value is insufficiently internalised by many therapists who lay claim to be person-centred in their practices. As a result such people do not understand the implication of the value – namely that they are not free to intervene unilaterally or to direct when they are acting as counsellors. Furthermore they cannot expect to escape feelings of conflict or tension if they are obliged or drawn to adopt therapeutic procedures culled from other schools of thought where the belief in *abdicating power in order to empower* is not a central tenet.

The inherent growth principle, the conditions for therapeutic movement and the supporting assertions offered by Bozarth and Temaner Brodley together constitute a powerful set of propositions for the person-centred counsellor, and this is summarised in Box 1.9. A counsellor who feels unable to subscribe to these propositions is unlikely to be able to practise person-centred counselling as we understand the term in this book.

Box 1.9 Propositions Central to Person-Centred Counselling

The person-centred counsellor affirms:

that every individual has the internal resources for growth;

that when a counsellor offers the core conditions of congruence, unconditional positive regard and empathy, she is creating the optimum conditions for therapeutic movement;

that human nature is essentially constructive;

that human nature is essentially social;

that self-regard is a basic human need;

that persons are motivated to seek the truth;

that perceptions determine experience and behaviour;

that the individual should be the primary-reference point in any helping activity;

that individuals should be related to as whole persons who are in the process of development;

that persons should be treated as doing their best to grow and to preserve themselves given their current internal and external circumstances;

that it is important to reject the pursuit of authority or control over others and to seek to share power.

'IT'S ALL ABOUT LOVING'

'Really, when you get down to basics, person-centred counselling is very simple. It's all about loving. It's about being free to treat other people in a loving way. It's trying to put the loving into helping.' This assessment, which appeared in a student's essay, would make many academics cringe. But essentially the student is right, for his conclusion does logically follow from even the most detailed analysis of the person-centred counsellor's propositions. What is more, person-centred counsellors in training can see that the process they are going through is one which is gradually freeing their 'loving' selves, with the first stage often being that of helping them to be able to 'love' themselves, to achieve the self-acceptance which they hope to facilitate in their clients.

It is easy to summarise the person-centred approach in this way, but it does not communicate what it looks like in action. The final box of this chapter (Box 1.10) attempts to convey something of the ethos and drama of the person-centred counsellor's work. It is a kind of 'trailer' for much that will follow later in the book.

Box 1.10 Jean and Jim

It is the beginning of Jean's second session with her client, Jim. Both of them are sitting on similar chairs. They are more or less facing each other and Jean, looking relaxed, opens with: 'What would you like to start with today, Jim?'

Jim takes up this invitation and starts to describe the very involved, often contradictory feelings he has about the fact that his wife has recently left him and taken their three children with her.

Jean looks *very* attentive – as though she's really straining to understand as fully as she can.

At one point Jean says: 'I see now that I wasn't really understanding you fully last week. I saw your anger, your dejection, your confusion, but today I see your real *desperation* . . . your real fear . . . fear of . . .'

This helps Jim to go on to talk about how his whole future seems to have become blank . . . How he used to be able to see clearly, and how now it is just a fog . . . He shivers . . . He is very scared. Jean reaches out and holds his hand. He cries.

The scene shifts to a few sessions later. Jim is not 'better'. He has become more depressed. It is now obvious that his wife has made a definite and seemingly permanent break. Jim is very quiet.

Jean catches his fleeting glance and says: 'You seem very far away today, Jim – what's going on in you?'

There is a very long silence but it is obvious that it is Jim's silence. He is probably running around in his mind. He takes a packet of cigarettes from his pocket, but does not open it. He turns it around in his hand – looking at it from all sides. Then he speaks: 'It's like this is my life . . . and I am looking at it . . . I'm looking at it very, very carefully . . . I am deciding whether I want it . . . or not.'

At that point, in an off-hand way, Jim tosses the packet of cigarettes across the room.

Jean shivers . . . and is slow to respond. She was already sitting forward in her seat, but moves further forward, and says: 'How does it look?'

This session goes on far beyond the normal hour and consists of Jean being a 'companion' to Jim's exploration of whether or not he

---

Box 1.10 continued

wants his life. At the end of the session Jim, still apparently undecided, says how important it is 'to really be able to choose'.

At no time during these exchanges has Jean been concerned to offer interpretations of Jim's behaviour, nor has she used any 'exercises' with him. In particular, she has not attempted to impose any of her own, or society's, values on him.

She has empathised a lot and been free to show her warmth. She has seemed spontaneous and genuinely non-judgemental. She has appeared quite comfortable, apart from the shiver, in the coldest parts of Jim's affective world. She has moved around in that world without seeming threatened by its intensity, its despair, and the possibility that Jim might make another choice about his life.

It goes without saying that no two counsellors, even from the same tradition, will respond in exactly the same way. This is particularly true in the person-centred approach which emphasises the uniqueness not only of the client, but of the counsellor. Nevertheless, the last paragraph of Box 1.10, describing Jean's behaviour, consistently reflects the person-centred approach in action with evidence of the three basic conditions of empathy, unconditional positive regard and congruence.

One interesting thing is that some counsellors from other traditions would recognise Jean's responses to Jim as close to their own. That is as it should be. Research suggests that experienced counsellors of different traditions are in broad agreement on the fact that the *relationship* between client and counsellor is of fundamental importance in counselling (for example Fiedler, 1950; Howe, 1993). The distinctive feature about the person-centred approach is that it does not just pay lip service to the importance of the relationship, but actually takes that as the aim of the counselling process with *every* client. In the person-centred approach there is no withdrawal from the relationship and retreat into exercises, interpretation or analysis of the client's behaviour. The relationship is *all*-important: if that is healthy then the counselling outcome has the best chance of being productive. It is the counsellor's responsibility to try to create that healthy relationship through her empathy, her basic valuing and unconditional acceptance of the client as a person of worth, and her congruence or authenticity. Such skills and attitudes are not easy to develop. Fortunately, once developed, they are not easy to lose.

2

THE COUNSELLOR'S USE OF THE SELF

A HARD DISCIPLINE

It has sometimes been suggested that of all the counselling disciplines the person-centred approach places the most rigorous demands upon its practitioners. There is no way of proving or disproving this assertion but certain factors indicate that it is by no means a fanciful idea. The person-centred counsellor knows that she cannot rely upon her diagnostic skill, her role as a provider of 'treatment', or a sense of superiority at being regarded as an all-knowing 'expert'. Instead each new client presents a fresh challenge to her humanity and to her ability to enter into a relationship where she can be accepting, empathic and authentic. Every new encounter brings with it, therefore, the prospect of an intimate meeting, together with all the unpredictable joys and stresses which are an inevitable part of any human relationship that moves beyond the superficial. This investment of the self of the counsellor in the therapeutic process cannot be over-emphasised. Often professional helpers are conditioned not to become 'involved' with their clients and advised to remain objective or even gently aloof. Such guidance is firmly rejected by the person-centred counsellor, who believes that it is precisely her ability to become involved and to share her client's world which will determine her effectiveness. The nature and quality of the involvement, and what this means for the counsellor's relationship with herself, are the subjects of this chapter. It will become evident that person-centred counselling is not the kind of activity to be undertaken by someone who rapidly tires of self-exploration or who wishes to avoid the pain of vulnerability.

THE SELF-LOVE OF THE COUNSELLOR

The world is full of helpers whose activity is a desperate strategy to avoid confronting themselves. This self-evasion is sometimes mistaken for self-lessness and can receive reinforcement from a misguided understanding of the Christian tradition where the concepts of selfishness and self-love have often become hopelessly confused. According to this misunder-standing one's own needs must always be subordinated to the needs of the other and it is considered unhealthy even to reflect unduly on one's own state of being. Once such a way of thinking is allied to a common distrust of introspection the scene is well set for the kind of helping which is per-meated by a dogged sense of martyrdom and further damages the self-respect of the person being helped. For the person-centred counsellor the ability to love herself is, in fact, the cornerstone for her therapeutic practice, and in its absence the usefulness of the helping relationship will be grossly impaired. It is impossible to offer a client acceptance, empathy and genuineness at the deepest level if such responses are withheld from the self.

Self-love is not easily attained and it needs frequent tending once estab-lished. Essentially it requires a willingness to give oneself time, attention and care, not out of self-indulgence but from a sense of responsibility to clients in the service of the work of counselling. Often this will mean a preparedness to seek out, on a consistent basis, the support of a friend or colleague with whom it is possible to be open, vulnerable and confused. This may or may not be the same person who provides regular consulta-tive support for the counselling work in progress. In the person-centred tradition, however, it is common for the work in supervision to include attention to the ongoing personal development of the counsellor. When the quality of the counsellor's being is such a fundamental factor in the creation of the therapeutic conditions this is perhaps not altogether sur-prising. The relationship which the counsellor has with herself will, to a large extent, determine the quality of the work she is able to initiate with clients, and is therefore a natural subject for a supervisor's attention.

LISTENING TO THE SELF

Self-love runs the risk of being no more than self-deception if it is not solidly anchored in self-knowledge. The counsellor therefore needs to cul-tivate the capacity to listen to herself, especially when such listening threatens to be painful or confusing. Not only is such an ability crucial to the development of self-awareness but it is also a basic aspect of the congruence or authenticity which will subsequently be offered to clients. For many people such listening is best undertaken in the presence, and with the help, of another person – whether therapist, supervisor or friend – but this is by no means the only arena for the development of such an ability. For some the practice of meditation or certain forms of prayer can be equally productive (and revealing) while yet others will best listen to themselves when they go walking alone or simply stand and stare at a scene of natural beauty. The chances are, however, that such opportunities will need to be deliberately and consciously sought and planned. The frenetic world in which most of us live is full of noise, distraction and perturbation. In such a context it can become increasingly difficult to listen to one's own thoughts, feelings and intuitions, and all too easy to lose contact altogether with the inner world which is the counsellor's most precious resource. There are those who can benefit from a structured approach to self-exploration and it is possible to devise one's own simple exercises to facilitate 'tuning-in' to the deeper layers of the self. Simple and direct questions such as: What is giving me most happiness these days? What is causing me most pain? What do I yearn for most? can, for example, provide ample scope for hours of profitable reflection. The method known as 'focusing', developed by Eugene Gendlin and discussed in Chapter 3, is a more sophisticated elaboration of the same kind of approach. There are some counsellors, too, who derive much benefit from the disciplined keeping of a daily journal which focuses not on external events but upon states of mind and the world of the feelings. Such journals can also be a natural repository for the recording of significant dreams and their exploration. In short the possible modes for listening to the self are many and varied. There is no lack of ways and means. What is required, however, is the person-centred counsellor's determination to submit to the discipline which each and every approach demands (see also Thorne, 1994).

SELF-ACCEPTANCE

Listening to the self is one thing. Coming to terms with what one hears is an altogether different matter. Those who take time out each year to spend some days apart, perhaps in a Retreat House or in a solitary spot, seldom find such occasions comfortable or reassuring. In the deeper levels of the self there is not infrequently a gnawing unease, a lack of contentment, a restlessness which is often accompanied by feelings of self-criticism that can easily tip over into self-disgust. And yet the person-centred counsellor is in the business of acceptance. Not to be self-accepting is to entertain a contradiction at the very centre of the therapeutic enterprise. Self-acceptance should not be confused with complacency or a kind of weary resignation. The complacent or resigned person has usually called a halt to self-exploration so that he can rest on his laurels or give up the effort. He can then turn a deaf ear and a blind eye to the responses of those around him. Such a person is no longer growing and is unlikely to assist the development of others. Self-acceptance is without meaning or value unless it is accompanied by the desire for growth and a willingness to face the truth. Unfortunately the truth about ourselves often involves feelings of guilt and it is then that self-acceptance seems a particularly difficult accomplishment.

Guilt itself is a complex emotion and can conceal many different origins. Undoubtedly there is a guilt which springs from having failed to fulfil someone else's expectations or come up to their (usually high) standards. Such guilt can produce deep feelings of failure or depression which in turn sow the seeds of self-rejection. The tragic side of such a process is that most often the goals or standards which have not been reached have significance to the individual only in so far as their non-attainment deprives him of the approval of those who set the goals in the first place. In this sense the guilt is actually misplaced, for it does not belong to the world of the individual's own deepest desires and aspirations. A young man feels guilty, for example, because he has not become the successful accountant his father expected him to be. In his misery he overlooks the fact that he does not wish to be an accountant at all, let alone a successful one. Until this tangle can be sorted out the young man has little chance of attaining the kind of self-acceptance which is independent of criteria established by others. In person-centred terms the misplaced guilt springs from failing to fulfil the conditions of worth imposed by others. This is different from guilt feelings arising from a betrayal of the self – where there is a sense of having let *oneself* down, of having failed in some way to fulfil the meaning of one's own existence.

Misplaced guilt scarcely calls for forgiveness. It requires instead a process of clarification, a tracking down of its origins and, in this way, a reduction of its power or, at best, its extinction. Guilt which arises from self-betrayal calls for compassionate patience on the part of the one who experiences it, a willingness not to condemn oneself because the flower of the personality has not yet bloomed. Counsellors learn to wait patiently for change in their clients but often find it difficult to extend to themselves the same forebearance. And yet the failure to do so makes their acceptance of their clients' slowness or resistance to change an act, at the deepest level, of patronising tolerance.

If self-acceptance is a primary obligation for the person-centred counsellor then its continuing achievement deserves the most thorough commitment. Listening to the self can sometimes be accomplished alone, but it is much less likely that self-acceptance will be achieved simply by communing with oneself. Not that this is totally impossible, especially if an inner dialogue can be established in which the compassionate part of the self can engage with the punitive or judgemental part and find itself heard. Some people even manage to facilitate a kind of internal discussion group in which various facets of the self are allowed to have their say until a co-operative harmony is established which makes it possible for the person to let go of the shame or the feelings of unworthiness which had originally been induced by the strident utterances of the judgemental self. Such internal reconciliation is rarely achieved this way, however, and then usually only by those who can hold in their minds the knowledge of those whose certain love and acceptance they have enjoyed in the past.

For most of us self-acceptance is much more likely to be maintained if we can take the risk of expressing our self-disgust and our self-reproachfulness in the presence of others who are prepared to take our misery seriously without colluding with the condemnation which we inflict upon ourselves. In practice, this means that the person-centred counsellor does well to participate in a group where it is permissible to articulate feelings of inadequacy, incompetence, hopelessness and shame in the knowledge that such feelings will be respected and understood, and will not be taken as signs of weakness or professional uselessness. Such groups are not easily come by and seldom exist within institutions or agencies however much such organisations may boast of their 'support' groups. Only too often these so-called support groups turn out to be yet another setting for helpers to indulge in a subtle competitiveness where they conceal their feelings of worthlessness behind a smokescreen of professional effectiveness. Self-acceptance will be achieved and maintained in a group where it is safe to be vulnerable and where the vulnerability extends to admitting the feelings of self-disgust and self-rejection. Such feelings are disarmed and transformed when they meet not pity or contempt but acceptance and understanding.

THE DEVELOPMENT OF EMPATHY

Self-acceptance is certainly strengthened when the counsellor experiences not only the understanding of others but the increasing range of her own empathic capacities. Empathy should not be confused with sympathy. Whereas sympathy arises from feeling compassionately moved by the experience of another, and to some extent sharing in it, empathy requires the much more complex and delicate process of stepping into another person's shoes and seeing the world through his or her eyes without, however, losing touch with one's own reality. Such a capacity is likely to be fostered by making the deliberate effort to move outside the confines of one's normal social environment or subgroup. The counsellor does well to encounter those of whom she has little knowledge or those by whom she feels threatened or intimidated. The benefits of this broadening of social experience go far beyond a simple increase in understanding of the actual people and groups she meets. In more general terms it tends to increase confidence and also humility, both of which facilitate the development of empathy.

Parochialism is the enemy of empathy but is as much a matter of attitude as of geography. Essentially it is the imagination which needs to be stimulated and enriched if the counsellor's empathic ability is to develop. It is in this respect that the discipline of psychology seems only rarely to provide the appropriate nourishment. On the contrary much psychological writing, in its attempt to convey the impression of objective scientific enquiry, oppresses the spirit by its laborious pedestrianism. Exceptions to this occur when attempts are made to explore subjective experience through the application of more humanistic paradigms, but such attempts are only recently beginning to grow with the increase in qualitative research projects. The person-centred counsellor is more likely to find food for the imagination in the works of novelists, poets and dramatists, and a good case could be made for requiring counsellors in training to make in-depth studies of some of the world's greatest creative writers. The counsellor who never reads a novel or never opens a book of poetry is neglecting an important resource for empathic development.

LEARNING TO BE GENUINE

The counsellor's ability to be genuine in her therapeutic encounters will be related to the way she conducts herself generally in her social relationships. There is something not a little spine-chilling about the counsellor who has the apparent capacity to 'turn on' her genuineness at the moment when the therapeutic hour begins, as if congruence were some kind of behavioural technique which can be applied when required. The implications of genuineness in a therapeutic relationship are discussed at length later in the book, but at this stage our concern is to look briefly at the 'way of being' which will characterise the counsellor's total existence and not simply her professional activity. This 'global' perspective is perhaps nowhere more relevant than in the consideration of what it means to be genuine in one's human interactions.

Learning to be genuine is usually a gradual process involving a dedicated and enduring commitment from the person-centred counsellor. She will delicately experiment with her genuine reactions to people and events and welcome feedback on the way others perceive her. Inevitably this 'testing' of herself is not restricted to the counselling context and other friends, colleagues and, most particularly, her loved ones might notice the difference as she gradually becomes more trusting of herself and consequently more able to be genuine even in difficult situations. Often the counsellor's evolution will be valued by those around her. For example, the counsellor who is a mother may begin to show her loving feelings more spontaneously towards her children; she may become more immediate in her intimate contact with her partner, and perhaps she will participate more actively and fully in family activities. However, there are likely to be other consequences of the counsellor's developing genuineness. She will probably become less guarded about her other not-so-loving feelings towards her children, more forthright in expressing difficulties with her partner and more determined in asserting her right to devote energy and time to interests outside the family.

All these outcomes of the counsellor's developing genuineness are changes, and change, whatever shape it takes, can upset the delicate balances and patterns within relationships. Such shifts can bring opportunities for the enhancement of relationships but like any change they carry some danger as well. For example, counsellors in training occasionally report a heightening of emotional, including sexual, expressiveness. It is easy to see how such an effect might be enhancing for the counsellor's relationship with her partner, but even such an apparently positive change might prove threatening and unwelcome in some cases.

THE 'HEALTHY RELATIONSHIP' BETWEEN COUNSELLOR AND CLIENT

All that has been said so far points to the central importance of the relationship which the counsellor has with herself. Can she be self-loving and self-accepting? Can she discipline herself enough to seek consciously for ways of extending her empathic abilities? Can she trust herself enough to give expression to her own self and to risk genuineness with her intimates? It is the answers which the counsellor gives to questions of this nature (see Box 2.1) which will to a large extent determine whether or not she is capable of offering a 'healthy' relationship to her clients. Before proceeding to explore the nature of this 'healthy' relationship it should be emphasised again, however, that person-centred counselling is only one form of helping, and that there are many other forms which in no way require the kind of relationship with the self which has been described. Unempathic surgeons, for example, can do splendid work and it is well known that some of the world's greatest saints have brought untold blessings to others while remaining convinced of their own worthlessness. The healthy relationship which will now be explored concerns person-centred counsellors and their clients. It is not a template for all helping relationships, let alone for effective human relating in general.

If the person-centred counsellor is 'at home' with her inner world and comfortable with her way of being it is likely that her work with clients will be characterised by a number of factors which taken in sum point to a healthy therapeutic relationship as conceptualised in the person-centred tradition. Not all these factors will necessarily be present in every relationship, but they are likely to be discernible across the range of the counsellor's clientele and stem from the basic attitudes and beliefs which have been outlined in the opening chapter.

Box 2.1 Self-Questioning of the Person-Centred Counsellor

1 Can I distinguish between self-love and selfishness and commit myself to embrace the former?
2 Am I self-accepting?
3 Do I seek consciously to extend my empathic skills?
4 Can I be genuine enough to disclose my thoughts and feelings to my friends and intimates, especially when I am feeling angry or resentful, weak or unlovable?

The counsellor's concern to relate to her client on a basis of equality, and not to get caught in the role of the diagnostic or treatment expert, means that she will do all in her power to demystify the counselling process. She will be as open as possible about her purposes and will not seek to evade direct questions which a client may pose as he struggles to decide whether or not to embark on a counselling relationship. She will be prepared, if need be, to discuss with the client the underpinning rationale of person-centred counselling and she will be likely to stress the co-operative nature of the activity. She will indicate either explicitly or implicitly that she has no intention of taking responsibility *for* the client but that she will do her utmost to be responsible *to* him by committing herself to establishing a relationship in which he can explore his concerns in an environment of support and understanding. This openness about purposes and intentions is the first and necessary sign of a healthy relationship and usually does much at the outset to 'dethrone' the counsellor and to establish a situation where the client recognises rapidly that he has to take his fair share of responsibility for his current predicament and for the changes which will be necessary if movement is to occur.

It is important both at this early stage and as counselling proceeds that the counsellor monitors continually what she is prepared to offer to the client, and what lies outside the boundaries of her commitment. There will be no decreed limits about this and a counsellor's preparedness to offer of herself and of her energies may vary widely between clients and with the same client at different stages of the counselling process. What is of crucial importance, however, if a relationship is to remain healthy, is that the counsellor is as clear as possible about what she is willing to deliver and that the client is appraised of this. Some counsellors fall unwittingly into the trap of offering the moon, and are then surprised or distressed at the client's increasing disappointment and resentment when the moon is not forthcoming. Where there is a lack of openness and a failure to spell out the extent of the commitment it is also possible for a client to fantasise in ways which are potentially damaging and often hurtful. The fantasies can differ dramatically. For one client there may be a permanent fear of being cast out at the end of the session, or before the next appointment, simply because the counsellor has not addressed the question of the duration of the counselling or of how it will eventually be terminated. For another there may be the growing fantasy that the counsellor has fallen in love with him and will never leave him. How otherwise could she treat him so kindly and offer him such sensitive understanding? It is only through a preparedness to be open and explicit about purpose and commitment that such fantasies can be confronted, and often it is only through continual reiteration by word and behaviour on the part of the counsellor that they can finally be dispelled.

The person-centred counsellor has nothing to gain by being anything other than transparent to her client. She does not profess to know what is 'good for' the client, and is not therefore concerned to exercise manipulatory skills, however well intentioned, in order to achieve 'good' outcomes. It is an indication of a healthy relationship when there is little preoccupation with 'progress' on the part of the counsellor because she knows that she is not the appropriate arbiter of this. Indeed, it is often amusing to discover that what may seem like a remarkable lack of progress to the counsellor may be seen quite differently by the client who, after all, has access to yardsticks for judgement of whose very existence the counsellor may be unaware (see Box 2.2). It is somewhat less amusing to acknowledge that counsellors who believe themselves to be highly successful would often have a rude shock if they consulted their clients, and if the latter felt courageous enough to speak the truth.

Box 2.2 Who Knows What Is 'Progress'?

The following is an extract from a taped counselling session where the counsellor has just expressed uncertainty and curiosity about what benefit the client has been drawing from their seven sessions thus far.

CLIENT: . . . What have I been getting out of it? Wow! . . . It has just kept me alive, that's all! I often go round and round in circles when I'm with you, and it seems like I'm getting nowhere, but all the time I'm *being me*: I'm being what I can't risk with anyone else − I'm being confused, distraught . . . crazy. I mean I know now that I'm not crazy . . . but I didn't know that before. It feels like the more I can just be these things with you, then the less frightened I am of them . . . the less frightened I am of me.

If the counsellor's lack of interest in manipulating her clients to 'good' ends is the mark of a healthy relationship, so too is her preparedness to *be* manipulated and even on occasions to be taken for a ride by an apparently scheming client. The person-centred counsellor, it will be recalled, has a basic trust in human nature and believes that there is in each one of us a desire for the truth and for constructive social intercourse. Such a belief does not mean that the counsellor is gullible and blind to human perversity, but it does imply that she is prepared to trust those who are manifestly untrustworthy so that they may gradually discover their own trustworthiness. In a strange way therefore the counsellor's willingness to allow herself to be deceived is again a mark of the relationship's health. The counsellor does not attempt to catch the client out, nor does she continually question the client's motives. She accepts that the client is doing his best, given his particular circumstances, to grow and to protect himself, and if this means that for the time being he has to manipulate and deceive her then she is prepared to stay with him through such deception rather than enjoy the dubious pleasure of unmasking him and preserving her own pride. By showing that she is not interested in playing power games or in scoring points the counsellor hopes that the client will gradually no longer have need to resort to deceit and manipulation in order to preserve his frail identity. Such behaviour will fall away once the client feels the safety of a relationship where he is respected despite his initial inability to reciprocate such respect.

The willingness to submit to manipulation if need be is but one sign of the counsellor's determination to stay with her client through thick and thin. A healthy relationship will not be undermined by the client's hostility or defensiveness nor by the counsellor's own feelings of dislike for the client. Instead it will be characterised by a preparedness to 'fight' for the relationship in the sense of offering a solid commitment which can transcend difficulties of understanding and withstand the unpredictable vagaries of the client's moods and doubts. There will, of course, be the occasional relationship where the counsellor's feelings of dislike or even outright hostility for the client are of such intensity and duration that they have to be expressed if genuineness is to be preserved. Such expression, however, will again be a sign of the counsellor's commitment to the relationship and her willingness to face her own pain and the negativity engendered by the interaction with the client. Often, indeed, the expression of such feelings immediately moves the relationship on to a new level of intimacy, or, at worst makes for the possibility of an appropriate referral to another counsellor. There is no sense in which a counsellor will give voice to her dislike in order to evade responsibility and commitment, or in the hope of getting rid of a tiresome and unco-operative client.

This preparedness to go to almost inordinate lengths to make manifest the commitment to the client is of crucial significance to those people whose life experience has taught them to expect rejection, fickleness and a lack of dependability in others. At the same time the counsellor must take care that her desire to indicate her commitment is not perceived by the client as an imposition or an unwelcome intrusion. The tight-rope that sometimes has to be walked is often revealed when a particularly shy or self-rejecting client fails to appear for an appointment after a difficult previous session. Such people are prone to see themselves as 'unworthy' clients, as if their struggles in the counselling relationship are yet another sign of inadequacy to add to the long list of their previous failures. On the other hand it is possible that there is a reason for their absence which has nothing to do with such feelings of inadequacy. The counsellor is faced with a dilemma. Does she do nothing, thus possibly giving the message to the client that she does not really care whether he comes or not, or does she make contact and run the risk of being perceived as an interferer or a 'possessive' counsellor? If she is working in private practice does she simply send the client the bill for this missed appointment without comment? In practice it is likely that most person-centred counsellors will write to such a client in a way which attempts to convey the counsellor's continuing commitment while giving the client absolute freedom to make up his own mind what to do next. Letters of this kind are often difficult to compose and will clearly vary from one client to another. An example of such a 'tight-rope' note appears in Box 2.3. In some cases a client who receives such a letter may make no response in the short term and may seem to have disappeared without trace. Not infrequently, however, such a person will renew contact many months later and will express gratitude both for the counsellor's expression of commitment and for the 'permission' to opt out of counselling for a while.

Box 2.3 Commitment Without Imposition

Dear Michael,
I was sorry not to see you for your appointment today and I do hope things are not too difficult. Do not hesitate, will you, to 'phone in to book another appointment if you would like that. It goes without saying that I shall be very pleased indeed to see you but shall quite understand if you wish to stop for the moment. With best wishes,

Yours,
Jean.

It is a popular misconception that a counselling process will invariably be of comparatively short duration. There are certainly many cases where five or six sessions will be sufficient to help the client along his road, and even times when one cathartic session may clear the air enough for the client, who then prefers to continue on his own. However, there are many clients whose concerns are such that they desire contact over many months or even years as they gradually reorient themselves and their living. In cases such as these the counsellor's willingness to 'fight' for the healthy relationship is a vital ingredient, lest the couple fall into a pattern of relating which is 'comfortable' rather than dynamic, or worse, a pattern which ensnares the client and reinforces his impotence. A sure indication of the counsellor's determination to 'fight for' the healthy relationship is her scrupulous attentiveness to the process so as to ensure that her commitment to her client does not result in a subtle abuse of power which can land the client in a kind of compassionate prison from which he feels unable to escape without wounding the kindly gaoler. Box 2.4 shows such attentiveness in action. In many ways the person-centred counsellor's firm commitment to her client and her equally strong desire that the client shall be free to find his own way forward are the two primary reference points for her way of being in this relationship. In different ways, and with varying degrees of emphasis, she will be attempting to say:

I am willing to invest myself in this relationship with you and to let you see me as I am. At the same time I make this investment without strings attached. You are free to be you and to leave this relationship when you wish. I am committed to stay with you for as long as that commitment enhances your development, but when it ceases to do so I shall be equally committed to helping you to leave me.

Box 2.4 Commitment not Entrapment

COUNSELLOR: We have been working together for some six months now and I am aware that much has changed for you. I wonder how you are feeling about where we have got to.

CLIENT: A long way to go, I reckon, but perhaps I can let go your hand soon.

COUNSELLOR: A few more weeks and then . . .

CLIENT: That's how it feels at the moment.

Letting be and letting go is not an altogether inadequate way to attempt to summarise the person-centred counsellor's complex and demanding task. It is in the service of this task that she strives to offer the 'healthy relationship' whose major characteristics are listed in Box 2.5.

Box 2.5 Characteristics of the 'Healthy' Therapeutic Relationship

1 The counsellor is open about her purposes.
2 The counsellor is responsible *to* her client and not *for* him.
3 The counsellor does not manipulate her client but is prepared to be manipulated.
4 The counsellor does not profess to know what is 'good' for the client.
5 The counsellor is not oriented towards 'success'.
6 The counsellor is clear about what she is willing to offer the client at every stage.
7 The counsellor is committed to the client and will 'fight' for the relationship.
8 The counsellor is prepared to invest herself in the relationship without strings attached.
9 The counsellor desires the client's freedom to be himself.

THE UNIQUE SELF OF THE COUNSELLOR

It is self-evident that person-centred counsellors, however much they may adhere to the same underlying principles which govern their counselling relationships, will vary widely in temperament and in personal attributes. The authors of this book are no exception. One is a somewhat intellectual and literary Englishman, sometimes to be found sniffing incense in Anglo-Catholic churches with a furled umbrella on his arm, while the other is a no-nonsense Scotsman initially schooled in the hard sciences, whose idea of fun is braving the rapids to ensnare an unsuspecting trout. These two very contrasting personalities clearly bring different attributes and widely differing life experiences to their counselling relationships. As person-centred counsellors our concern is to ensure that our unique strengths – and weaknesses, for that matter – can be invested in our therapeutic work to the benefit of our clients. In short, we both wish to be ourselves in our work and are therefore anxious to make *all* our relevant attributes available to our counselling relationships, where this is appropriate. We do not wish to be confined to a narrow array of therapeutic responses as if acceptance, empathy and genuineness can only be communicated in certain stereotyped ways. Each counsellor has her own unique repertoire and the therapeutic enterprise will be much enriched if she is able to exploit such a repertoire to the full and to make appropriate use of her own particular talents.

A counsellor's special gifts may not always be apparent in the early years of practice. There is a sense in which the preoccupation with 'doing a good job' ensures a conscientious adherence to the 'norms' of the approach and a wholly appropriate emphasis on establishing the core conditions. The counsellor is likely to do her utmost to convey acceptance to her client and to track his inner world with all the empathic skill at her command. She will also be at pains not to put up a professional mask behind which she can take refuge when the going gets tough. It is unlikely, however, that as a fledgling counsellor she will be bold enough to take the kind of risks which are involved if a deeper level of her own personality is to be put at the service of her client. It is only when she feels a growing security in her own capacity to function as a 'good enough' counsellor that she is likely to discover and then to offer those attributes which constitute her own uniqueness.

In the case of one of us (Thorne) it was some years before it became possible to identify a particular quality of being and then to recognise this as of fundamental importance in many therapeutic encounters (Thorne, 1985, 1991a). Today, however, this quality of tenderness, as he has come to describe it, is an important expression of particular gifts which spring from his unique personality and experience. The implications of these gifts for the counselling process have been explored elsewhere (Thorne, 1987) but for our present purposes it is relevant to focus on the experience of the counsellor himself as he came to trust parts of his own being which had not previously had much of an entrée into his counselling work. It makes sense for Brian Thorne to take up his own story.

TAKING RISKS WITH THE UNIQUE SELF

For many years I had been aware that with certain clients I often felt an almost overwhelming sense of interrelatedness. Such clients varied widely in background and life experience and were often not people with whom I might have expected a natural affinity. My immediate reaction to such feelings was to distrust them and to suspect that some process of projection or counter-transference was taking place, of which I should take note and then proceed with the utmost caution.

One day, however, for I know not what reason, I decided to throw such caution to the winds. I suppose at some level I reminded myself that I was not a counsellor in the analytic tradition but someone who believed in the fundamental trustworthiness of human beings, and that this category included myself. I knew that I was an experienced and responsible counsellor and that I was committed to my client's well-being. My own congruence – the outcome of the discipline of my chosen therapeutic approach – was revealing to me a strong sense of being intimately involved at a profound level with someone with whom I apparently had little in common. I decided to trust that feeling, however mysterious or inexplicable, and to hold on to it rather than dismissing it or treating it with my usual circumspection. The result of that decision has been far-reaching, for I discovered that my trust in this sense of profound interrelatedness (and it usually happens quite unpredictably) gives access to a world which seems outside of space and time and where it is possible for both my client and me to relate without fear and with astonishing clarity of perception. I have attempted to give some sense of this experience as follows:

> My client seems more accurately in focus: he or she stands out in sharp relief from the surrounding decor. When he or she speaks, the words belong uniquely to him or her. Physical movements are a further confirmation of uniqueness. It seems as if for a space, however brief, two human beings are fully alive because they have given themselves and each other permission to risk being fully alive. At such a moment I have no hesitation in saying that my client and I are caught up in a stream of love. Within this stream there comes an effortless or intuitive understanding and what is astonishing is how complex this understanding can be. It sometimes seems that I receive my client whole and thereafter possess a knowledge of him or her which does not depend on biographical data. This understanding is intensely personal and invariably it affects the self-perception of the client and can lead to marked changes in attitude and behaviour. For me as a counsellor it is accompanied by a sense of joy which when I have checked it out has always been shared by the client. (Thorne, 1985: 9)

It is clear to me now that the decision to trust the feeling of interrelatedness was the first step towards a willingness on my part to acknowledge my spiritual experience of reality and to capitalise on the many hours spent in prayer and worship. It was as if previously I had refused to draw on this whole area of awareness in the conduct of my therapeutic work. In my zeal not to proselytise it was as if I had deliberately deprived myself of some of my most precious resources in the task of relating to my clients. Once I had opened myself to myself, however, I was capable of experiencing the communion of souls, or the membership one of another, which is a fundamental given of the spiritual life. I still remain convinced, of course, that it is iniquitous to use a counselling relationship for evangelising. I am no more likely now to talk of God or religion in my counselling work than I was in earlier years. The difference is that I now attempt to be fully present to my clients, and this means that I do not leave my eternal soul outside the door. Interestingly enough, it has also meant that I am far less disembodied in my behaviour than I used to be. My acknowledgement of my spiritual self has led to the discovery that I can indeed use my whole self, including my physicality, through touching. When I am bold enough to accept my own uniqueness it seems that I am enabled to offer a tenderness which moves the soul while embracing (sometimes literally) the body. I admit to considerable embarrassment as I write these words, and yet I have come to believe that the person-centred counsellor has a particular obligation to be honest about all his or her attributes and to be prepared to acknowledge their potential contribution to the counselling relationship. For my own part I know that if I had continued to deny the therapeutic significance of some of the deepest parts of my own being I might never have tumbled to the fact that I have a capacity to express tenderness both physically and spiritually. Perhaps it is in the offering of this gift that I give the highest expression to my unique self, and that is why it always feels a risky undertaking where vulnerability and strength are present in equal measure. Nowadays, however, I know that I usually have no option but to take the risk. What is more, the risk has sometimes proved costly in terms of professional misunderstanding and even calumny (Thorne, 1996).

THE CHANGING SELF OF THE COUNSELLOR

Some twenty years ago Carl Rogers was asked to reflect on the experience of becoming old. He produced an article which he entitled 'Growing old', but before publication he modified the title to 'Growing old – or older and growing' (Rogers, 1980b). This anecdote enshrines an important precept

for the person-centred counsellor, and indeed for anyone engaged in therapeutic relationships. The work on the self can never be complete and the
counsellor is confronted by a lifetime's task if she is to remain faithful to
her commitment. If this sounds unduly demanding it needs to be remembered that counselling is about change and development, and that an
unchanging counsellor is well on the way to becoming a professional
charlatan. What is more, the counsellor's obligation to keep on growing is,
in fact, a glorious invitation to live life to the full. The person-centred
counsellor is challenged not so much to face the horrors of the unknown
(although some there may be) as to continue on a voyage of self-discovery
knowing that many of the most delectable places are yet to be visited.

3

EMPATHY

One of the central dimensions of the therapeutic relationship is *empathy*. Brief definitions seldom capture the full meaning of processes, but as a prelude to the more complete description offered in this chapter, the following might suffice:

> Empathy is a continuing process whereby the counsellor lays aside her own way of experiencing and perceiving reality, preferring to sense and respond to the experiences and perceptions of her client. This sensing may be intense and enduring with the counsellor actually experiencing her client's thoughts and feelings as powerfully as if they had originated in herself.

In the sequence reproduced in Box 3.1 the counsellor responds five times to the client, Bill. All these responses, including her touch on Bill's shoulder, are empathic responses in so far as they accurately reflect Bill's state of being in that moment.

It is difficult to extract examples of empathy from tapes of counselling sessions because empathy is not a single response made by the counsellor to the client. Nor is empathy fully encapsulated even by a series of responses as in Box 3.1. Rather than being a single response, or a series of responses, empathy is a *process*. It is a process of 'being with' the client.

Although we share the same physical world we all experience it in different ways, because we look at it from different perspectives or 'frames of reference'. In empathising with a client the counsellor leaves aside her

---

Box 3.1 Empathising with Bill, a Disillusioned Teacher

BILL: I guess I should have known that it wouldn't be that easy . . . . to just do it 'as a job', I mean . . . like I thought I could just 'disengage' and save myself.

COUNSELLOR: But you found that that didn't 'save' you – that it was just as bad or worse?

BILL: Yes, worse. I wouldn't have believed it could be worse. Like I thought that nothing could be worse than finding myself screaming at the kids and another time locking my door and crying by myself. But this is worse . . . like then at least I was alive.

COUNSELLOR: And now you're not.

BILL: Now I'm a zombie . . . in fact sometimes I'm worse than a zombie.

COUNSELLOR: . . . sometimes you're not even the *walking* dead?

BILL: Yes – now I often don't make it in – like I think of going in and I nearly vomit – maybe I'm school phobic – imagine that! . . .the teacher's school phobic! What a laugh [*laughs*]!

COUNSELLOR: Doesn't sound like you feel it's funny . . .

BILL: [*pause . . . starts to sob*].

COUNSELLOR: [*gently puts her hand on his shoulder and says nothing*].

---

own frame of reference and, for the time being, adopts the frame of reference of her client. She can then appreciate how the client experiences the events in his world; indeed she can even sense how he feels about events *as if* these feelings were her own. For example near the end of Box 3.1 Bill is laughing, but the counsellor knows that that is not all he is feeling. She has been in his frame of reference for some time and she knows that his feelings about school and his place in it are thoroughly desperate. She isn't just *thinking* about his feelings; it is likely that she too will be experiencing the same general 'tightness', or constricted throat that precedes his crying. She is experiencing Bill's feelings as if they were her own, but all the time the release of her empathic sensitivity is under her control: she does not 'get lost' in Bill's frame of reference, and can leave it whenever she wishes. The '*as-if*' quality of empathy is a crucial aspect of the professionalism of the person-centred counsellor. She is able to work in this intense and feelingful way with her client, and yet not become overwhelmed by those feelings. This control by the counsellor is crucial for the client: it offers him the security of knowing that although he may feel desperate and lost in his world, the counsellor will be someone who remains reliable and coherent, as well as sensitive.

Sometimes these particularly intense empathic experiences lead us to forget that in person-centred counselling empathy is going on most of the time and not just at profound moments. Right from the start of the relationship the counsellor endeavours to enter the client's frame of reference and walk alongside him in his world. When we are accompanying anyone on a journey we are likely to comment on what we see, and the same happens on an empathic 'journey'; the counsellor comments on what she sees. These comments are commonly called 'empathic responses'. The responses themselves are not 'empathy', but they are the products of the shared journey which is empathy.

Historically this notion of empathy as a process rather than a response has been much misunderstood. Researchers found it much easier to work with the quantifiable empathic response rather than the empathic process (Truax and Carkhuff, 1967; Carkhuff, 1971). Research based on logical positivism must necessarily restrict and reduce human processes in order to examine them. Unfortunately this narrow conception of empathy was not only used in research, but for many workers it became the basis for training in empathy. The result was that counsellors came to be trained in making empathic reflections on the false assumption that if they showed these limited behaviours, then empathy was taking place. In Box 3.2 the counsellor shows a reflection which looks empathic, but from this alone it is totally impossible to tell whether she is truly accompanying the client on his journey or simply responding with a 'stock' reflection.

In Box 3.2 the counsellor's response shows that she has heard the client's words, but the response is not likely to communicate with certainty that she fully understands what he is experiencing. This communication of accurate understanding is a vital part of the empathic response: the client must *feel* understood for empathy to have its impact.

Box 3.2 The Simple Reflective Response

CLIENT: Like I'm really flying in there – like flying through into that big black room. I'm not scared now . . . I like the dark . . .

COUNSELLOR: So you're going into that dark place . . . really fast . . . and it feels different . . . not scary now . . . even pleasant . . .

CLIENT: Yeah . . .

If research is to examine the *process* of empathy, then it must take into account not only the verbal response of the counsellor, and how this is perceived by the client, but also the interaction sequence which has led up to that response and the shared understandings which have been built up in previous sessions. If research truly considers all this relevant behaviour then it may begin to encompass the *process* nature of empathy. Otherwise it is an oversimple reductionist pastime which can only look at the 'communication skill' aspect of empathy.

In summary, then, empathy is not a 'technique' of responding to the client, but a way-of-being-in-relation to the client. Empathy often feels like being on the same train, or camel, as the client! It is the client's journey which the counsellor is joining and staying with, no matter how bumpy it is. Sometimes that journey feels smooth and at other times the traveller stops and starts, goes down blind alleys, gives up, and feels confused. Such journeys contain the same qualities of immediacy and intensity whether they are in the playroom with the six-year-old, in the locked ward with the schizophrenic, or in the student counselling office with the student who cannot decide whether or not to leave university. Empathy is like a cine-film whereas empathic responses are still photographs of that moving process. In the beginning, however, examining the stills is one place to start, and the trainee counsellor may well gain from exploring different examples of empathic responses.

An Empathy Scale

For such beginnings the notion of an *empathy scale* can be helpful. The empathy scale only focuses on the counsellor's empathic response, but it is a useful way of appreciating that there can be different degrees of empathic accuracy. For the skilled counsellor who is familiar with her client's paths, it is relatively easy to stay fully in the empathic process, but for the trainee counsellor, finding the paths of her client involves considerable effort, some successes, some failures and some partial successes. The empathy scale communicates this notion of hitting, missing and partially hitting.

Truax and Carkhuff (1967) developed sophisticated eight-point scales of empathy. These were used not only in research but also in training as a means of rating the level of empathy which the counsellor's response had exhibited on audio-taped interviews. Discussing these ratings, and the other possible responses the trainee counsellor might have made, could help to expand the trainee's repertoire of ways of communicating her empathy.

For our purposes a four-point empathy scale is sufficient to illustrate variety in empathic responses. On such a scale the different levels might represent the following:

Level 0   This is a response which shows no evidence of understanding of the client's expressed feelings. It may be a comment which is irrelevant to the client's feelings, or perhaps a judgemental response, advice-giving, hurtful or rejecting.

Level 1   This response shows only a partial understanding of those feelings and responses which are very much on the surface for the client. Sometimes this level of empathy is called 'subtractive' in the sense that the listener has lost something of the client's experience in the response she has fed back.

Level 2   In this response the listener is showing an understanding and acceptance of the feelings and thoughts which the client has been expressing. This level is sometimes called *accurate empathy*.

Level 3   This response shows an understanding of the client beyond the level of the client's immediate awareness. As well as communicating comprehension of the surface feelings and responses of the client, the listener is showing an understanding of *underlying* feelings. This is sometimes called 'additive' empathy, but is more commonly referred to as a *depth reflection*.

These different levels are illustrated by the following example from counselling practice. The actual response which the counsellor made was the one which is given at Level 3. However, as well as reproducing this response, we have constructed other possible responses which might indicate the different levels.

Example

In this extract the client is a mature student whose self-appraisal has grown considerably upon discovering that she is both a popular and a highly competent student. She had become very unhappy with the pattern in her relationship with her husband. Her statement is:

He treats me like a baby – looking after me all the time, mollycoddling me all the time . . . *suffocating* me! He fails to realise that since I've

come to university I am not such a baby any more . . . I'm
independent . . . I'm strong.

Possible responses at each of the four levels might be:

Level 0   *Men are all the same – you're better rid of them!* As well as being
an irrelevant and judgemental response which gives advice extremely
early, this response does not seem to show an understanding of the
client as a person. It is more the kind of response which a friend or
acquaintance might give if she does not really want the client to go
deeper into her feelings

Level 1   *God, that must be hard.* This response seems to show a partial
understanding of the client's feelings. At least the counsellor understands the seriousness and difficulty which the client is experiencing,
though the quality of her feelings is not being reflected in this 'subtractive' response

Level 2   *It's like he doesn't understand you . . . how you're changing . . . he
still treats you like he used to, which may have been OK then, but not
now . . . and you're damned angry at that.* Here the counsellor's response
is accurately reflecting back both the quality and the intensity of the
client's feelings. This sensitive response has not only taken into account
the client's words but has also encompassed the anger which was
clearly evident by the client gritting her teeth as she spoke. The fact that
the counsellor has pushed the client's response back to her in the counsellor's own words rather than hers is further confirmation of
understanding.

Level 3   *I see your anger that he doesn't understand that you're changing . . . that seems really really strong . . . but I also wonder . . . you look
as though you're trembling . . . is that trembling just your anger or is there
something else going on in you as well?* In the actual counselling session
from which this extract is taken, this response by the counsellor elicited
a long silence from the client as it touched the edge of her awareness.
Following this silence the client responded with what was to prove a
very powerful discovery: 'yes . . . yes, I'm scared . . . I'm scared I'll lose
him'. In this particular case the depth reflection proved important
since it helped the client become aware that not only was she *angry* at
her husband, but she was also extremely *scared* at the possibility of
their breaking up. The client later traced this fear to the fact that while
she was certainly becoming more and more independent, she was not
all the way along that road yet.

46

Sometimes the counsellor's attempts at a Level 3 empathic response will fall on stony ground. For instance, in the above example the client might have reflected on the counsellor's statement and replied: 'No, I'm just damned angry at him!' This response would indicate one of two things: either the counsellor was correctly sensing something underlying the surface feelings but the client was not yet able to become aware of it, or the counsellor was wrong. It does not really matter which of these is the case since the person-centred counsellor would be likely to drop it for the time being at least. Metaphorically, the person-centred counsellor wants to 'knock on the client's door' but she does not want to 'knock the door down'.

As we mentioned earlier, looking at empathic responses can be illuminating since they take a very concrete form, but it does carry the danger that the trainee counsellor might assume that there are 'perfect' responses which can suit any occasion. The response which the counsellor made at Level 3 in the above example very much fitted her relationship with that client. The client trusted and respected the counsellor, and was by no means overawed by her, but exactly the same response to exactly the same words of another client might not be empathic. In the example the power of empathy was there because the counsellor sensed something else at the edge of the client's awareness. *It was that sensing which was the empathy*. The words, that is to say, the 'empathic response', merely signposted the ongoing process of empathy. For trainee counsellors merely to rehearse responses like the one under consideration would be a totally meaningless activity, because they would have detached the words from the sensing. The words are not important: the same sensing which happened in the above example might have been communicated in a hundred different ways by the counsellor. For instance the counsellor might have leaned forward and held the client's hand in attentive silence. Such a non-verbal but powerful response might have helped the client to get in touch with the edge of her awareness.

The written word cannot adequately reproduce examples of empathy which involve the non-verbal, expressive behaviour of client and counsellor. The depth reflection relies a lot on the counsellor's sensitivity to the significance *for that client* of such expressive behaviour as a lowered head, a cracking voice, a clenched fist, a fixed gaze or a shiver. The client's whole communication consists of his words and his expressive behaviour. Sometimes these two aspects may even be giving different messages and the counsellor's depth reflection will likely reflect that difference; for example: 'You are *saying* that you are coping better now, but you also sound very tense . . . is it really OK now?' This issue of the client's contradictory

47

verbal and non-verbal behaviour is also explored in 'disguises and clues' in Chapter 6.

The counsellor's expressive behaviour is an important part of her empathic response, particularly in the case of depth reflections, for instance: the softness of her voice may be what reflects the quality of the client's experience more than the actual words the counsellor chooses, or perhaps it is the way the counsellor lowers her head, shows a faltering in her voice, clenches her fist, offers a fixed gaze, or shivers, which communicates the depth of her understanding.

While the depth reflection represents an alluring level of empathy, it is by no means the most frequent mode of response of the counsellor; responses at Levels 1 and 2 are much more common. At these levels the counsellor is showing a willingness to follow the consciousness of the client with varying degrees of success, while at Level 3 she is actually slightly ahead of that consciousness. Nevertheless Levels 1 and 2 are the 'meat and drink' of counselling sessions. They enable the counsellor and client to monitor the closeness of their journey. Even a response at Level 1 may be enough to show the client that the counsellor is willing and also struggling to understand, and often that willingness and struggle are appreciated as much as anything else.

Where the counsellor expresses only a *partial* understanding of the client's experience, more often than not the client then goes on to clarify that experience both for the counsellor and incidentally for himself, for instance:

CLIENT: I feel I am in a real bind with it. Like I can't give up the job because it's too risky – I just don't know what will happen – it could be really desperate. And on the other hand I can't stay in the job because it's slowly and steadily destroying me – and that destruction is getting really critical.

COUNSELLOR: So it's a really difficult decision to make?

CLIENT: It's not just that it's a difficult decision to make, it's an *impossible* decision to make – it's like I'm getting so desperate with fear that I can't move at all . . . It's like this is the first time I've ever seen hope for myself and the first time that I've ever thought seriously about leaving the job . . . And of course this is also the first time I've been so stuck in all my life.

In the above extract the counsellor had only shown a partial understanding of the intensity of the client's experience, but as often happens the client then helped them both along.

EMPATHY AND LOCUS OF EVALUATION

The person-centred counsellor is sensitive to her clients and their differences as well as to the influence of her own power. One important dimension of difference among clients is their 'locus of evaluation' described in Chapter 1. The counsellor using her sensitivity will find that she communicates her empathy quite differently to a client with an 'externalised' locus of evaluation compared to one whose locus is fairly 'internalised'. The client with an externalised locus is extremely vulnerable to the evaluations others place upon him. He is in the thoroughly frightening position of not being able to trust his judgements of himself; he cannot even trust his judgements of his own feelings. This can be a terrifying situation and one in which he desperately grasps hold of even the hint of an evaluation offered by another person. With this client, the counsellor's sensitivity would lead her to be wary of the potential invasiveness of her additive empathy. Most particularly she would not *name* any underlying feelings she might be experiencing in the client, for her client would have to accept these labels as truth – he would not have the reviewing and editing facility of the client whose locus of evaluation is more internalised. Furthermore, since an expected consequence of person-centred counselling is an internalising of the locus of evaluation, it makes more sense to encourage the client to exercise that facility rather than rely upon the counsellor's evaluations. Box 3.3 gives an example of the way the counsellor's responses would take into account the client's locus of evaluation. Further exploration of the importance of being sensitive to the client's locus of evaluation is provided in Mearns (1994: 80–3), where a link is drawn to the danger of inducing 'false memories' in such vulnerable clients.

Box 3.3 Empathy Sensitive to Locus of Evaluation

The client, Adrienne, has a profoundly externalised locus of evaluation – it is difficult for her to make judgements even about her own experiencing. We present her statement with possible responses from incompetent and competent counsellors.

ADRIENNE: I only have very hazy memories of what was, perhaps, 'abuse'. In fact, I don't even know that they *are* memories – maybe I'm just imagining them. I have feelings too, but they are all over the

---

49

Box 3.3 continued

place as well. I feel a lot of sadness – well, I cry a lot, so I imagine I must have a lot of sadness. I get frustrated a lot . . . but I'm not sure whether my frustration is at others or at me.

INCOMPETENT COUNSELLOR: How about anger? Is anger one of your feelings? [This person, who is trying to be a counsellor, has been on a course about 'adult survivors of childhood abuse'. She has learned that anger is often a repressed or suppressed emotion and that part of the process of healing is the client expressing that anger. Unfortunately, in the case of a client with an externalised locus of evaluation, this question is invasive and may lead the client to presume that she *must* be angry. The client may even feel worse about herself because she is unable to access this presumed anger.]

COMPETENT COUNSELLOR: Memories that may not be memories . . . crying that may be sadness . . . and frustration which may be at others or at yourself. What are you feeling *right now* . . . as you talk about this? [The person-centred counsellor is not directive about *what* the client is expressing but she may offer a 'process direction' (Rennie, 1998) which, in this case, invites the client to come into the present and focus upon her feelings in the moment. In so doing, the counsellor is also inviting the client to exercise herself as her locus of evaluation.]

WHY AND HOW IS EMPATHY IMPORTANT IN COUNSELLING?

The fact that empathy correlates with effective counselling is well established in research (Barrett-Lennard, 1962; Lorr, 1965; Truax and Mitchell, 1971; Gurman, 1977; Patterson, 1984; Sachse, 1990; Lafferty, Beutler and Crago, 1991; Burns and Nolen-Hoeksema, 1991; Orlinsky, Grawe and Parks, 1994). Such positive findings are consistent across countries (Tausch et al., 1970, 1972), and even within research studies examining other therapeutic approaches, for example cognitive therapy (Burns and Nolen-Hoeksema, 1991) and short term dynamic therapy (Vaillant, 1994). The significance extends not only to work with so-called neurotic clients but also to those with a schizophrenic diagnosis (Rogers et al., 1967). Indeed, in this last research, not only was a high level of accurate empathy related to a significant reduction in schizophrenic pathology, but those patients in relationships which were very low in empathy showed a slight *increase* in their schizophrenic pathology (pp. 85–6). This suggests not only that with profoundly disturbed clients the presence of empathy is helpful, but that counsellors who fail to create the empathic process may actually be damaging. This strong evidence for the importance of empathy is supported by the fact that practitioners across many counselling disciplines are agreed on its paramount importance (Fiedler, 1950; Raskin, 1974).

However, *why* empathy has such positive effects is more open to discussion. Certainly empathy communicates the counsellor's understanding of the client and this fact alone might increase the client's self-esteem ('Gosh, I'm understandable!'). Perhaps it is also the fact that, as we suggested in the opening chapter, the counsellor is willing to *struggle* to understand the client which contributes to its effect ('I am important enough for this person to struggle to understand me'). In a few cases the importance of empathy may be that it dissolves alienation, for it is almost impossible to maintain an alienated position in the face of someone who is showing you profound understanding at a very personal level.

It may be a somewhat cynical point of view, but in some cases the importance of the counsellor's empathy may have to do with the fact that the client has seldom experienced such a process with other helpers. ('Here's someone who's actually trying to understand me . . . someone who isn't just fitting me into her pet theories instead of really listening to me.')

If the reasons why empathy is effective can be varied, so too can the *process* by which it exerts its influence. Certainly one effect of empathy is that, by focusing on the client's surface and underlying feelings, his awareness of these is increased. Becoming aware of feelings which were earlier denied is the first step in taking responsibility for them and their implications. For instance, a wife might become aware of her underlying feelings of anger towards her husband, where formerly that anger had been denied in favour of 'irritation'.

Another consequence of empathy, which is well established in research, is that it tends to encourage further and deeper exploration on the part of the client (Tausch et al., 1970; Bergin and Strupp, 1972; Kurtz and Grummon, 1972). In other words, when the counsellor shows that she understands the feelings and thoughts being expressed by the client, a natural step for the client seems to be to unfold ever-deepening levels of his awareness. Obviously the feeling of being understood will contribute to this, but much of the effect might also be understood in terms of the conventions of conversation. When the counsellor attempts to re-formulate and reflect the client's process then implicitly at least there is an accompanying question: 'Is this an accurate understanding of you?' The conventions of conversation would demand a response from the client: if the counsellor has been even partially accurate in her response, then usually the client will take the discourse further, either to deepen or broaden it. A slight qualification is needed here, because it is possible to respond in such a definite, closing way that the client actually does stop – as though the counsellor has given the message that the whole episode is now closed. Indeed the same *words* can encourage closure if they are definite and conclusive, for instance: 'so you feel angry about that', or they can encourage further exploration if they are tentative and questioning: 'so . . . you feel . . . "angry" about that?' In delivering this as a tentative question the counsellor is not only checking her understanding but implicitly encouraging the client to move on by considering what else is present at the edge of his awareness. In so doing she is entering a particular area of expertise within empathy – focusing.

FOCUSING ON THE 'EDGE OF AWARENESS'

Already in this chapter we have referred to the terms *focusing* and *the edge of awareness*. In borrowing these terms we are recognising the striking contribution made by Eugene T. Gendlin to our understanding of the empathic process (Gendlin, 1981, 1984, 1996). Gendlin points out that often what is important is not the feeling which the client is currently experiencing about an event, but the underlying feelings and responses of which the client is not yet quite aware. Already in our examples of 'depth reflections' we have seen how significant underlying feelings can be. Sometimes such feelings are compatible with the current surface feeling and merely supplement it. However, on other occasions the underlying feeling might be quite opposite to what is experienced on the surface. For instance, a client may show superficial polite acquiescence towards an event while simultaneously, and not quite consciously, he is seething rebelliously underneath. At other times the underlying feeling is neither compatible with, nor opposite to, the surface feelings, but instead brings in a whole new way of looking at the event. For example, what seemed on the surface to be a difficulty in making a practical decision turns out to be concealing an intense fear of loss. In all these examples recognition of the underlying feeling is important for progress.

Gendlin takes this much further by pointing out that what is underlying our surface feelings cannot always properly be described as a feeling in itself – sometimes it is less clear and less intense than a feeling and is better described as a 'sensation'. It might be a sensation such as 'tightness', 'blackness', 'falling', 'a welling-up', 'stuckness', 'softness', or 'warmth'. Gendlin uses the term *felt sense* to talk about that edge of our awareness between the known and the unknown. The 'known' would be the client's surface feelings and other behavioural responses to the event, while the 'unknown' could include all sorts of deeper levels of feelings, associations with earlier events, or future aspirations. The known is readily available, but the unknown is not tapped simply by focusing on the known. Instead the appropriate focus is on the edge of awareness between the known and the unknown. Simply focusing on the known surface feelings may only be going over old ground, whereas focusing on 'the edge' (the felt sense) can be the door to the unknown. In Box 3.3 (pp. 49–50) the second 'counsellor' invited the client to focus upon the edge of her present awareness rather than staying at the level of 'rehearsed material', as Rogers called it (Rogers, 1977)

In her empathic journey with the client, the counsellor may frequently be attending to what the client is saying and the feelings which accompany that, but being fully *with* the client will imply that the counsellor is attending to, and checking on, the client's felt sense of the issue as well. The easy movement from one to the other is illustrated in Box 3.4. In this box both the counsellor and the client try to find what Gendlin calls *handle-words* to fit the felt sense. First the counsellor tries 'tightness' to describe the sensation epitomised by the client's screwing up of his face and body. The client tries out this handle 'tightness' by repeating it for himself. Gendlin talks about the client *resonating* the handle-word with the underlying sensation. In our extract the client then improves the handle-word to a 'screwing up' and then further improves it to 'being wound up'. At this point the client has reached his felt sense, which then opens the door to the fear expressed by his metaphor of the clockwork toy. In a very short time the client has gone from the known which was his excitement through his felt sense of being wound up to the unknown which was his fear that all his activity might make no difference to his life.

Sometimes handle-words take the form of *metaphors*, like the client's metaphor of the wind-up toy in Box 3.4. It is fascinating how metaphors often describe the quality and intensity of sensations more fully than single words. Even more amazing is the fact that metaphors can be culturally shared, for instance: *It feels as though the big boys have just stolen my new toy*. Almost universally, in western culture at least, this metaphor communicates a sense of loss far overshadowed by violation.

Box 3.4 Attending to the Client's Felt Sense

COUNSELLOR: You've made lots and lots of plans since we last met. I can see that you're excited by that . . . but is that all you feel? Do you feel anything else when you consider your plans?

CLIENT: [*pause*] No, I am just excited – and really looking forward to making a change [*pause*]. But [*long pause*] I do feel something else . . . but it's not very clear . . . it's a kind of [*screws up his face and his upper body*] . . .

COUNSELLOR: . . . a kind of . . . 'tightness'?

CLIENT: Yes – a tightness – a screwing up . . . like I'm being wound up like a children's wind-up toy – like I'm going to burst into action – frenetic action . . . and then maybe stop like the toy, and everything will be the same as it was [*he shivers violently*]!

Sometimes it is assumed that the use of metaphor is more associated with middle-class educated language. This is far from the truth, although the actual metaphors which are used to describe sensations can be quite different from one subculture to another. For example, it is illuminating to compare the following two metaphors:

It feels like being a Liverpool supporter at the Everton end.[1]
and
It feels like I'm the little girl that the other girls wouldn't speak to.

These two metaphors are similar but they are likely to belong to quite different subcultures. Learning to appreciate a wide range of metaphor is a very useful counsellor skill. It is just one of the ways in which the counsellor's breadth of life experience can contribute to her understanding of the varied 'personal languages' of clients, discussed in Chapter 4.

The felt sense of an issue can be likened to its *flavour* in that, whether we are focusing on the whole issue or only on a tiny part of it, the felt sense is the same. This quality of the felt sense is illustrated in Box 3.5.

Gendlin talks about the felt sense as residing 'in the middle of our body' (Gendlin, 1984: 78) (here there are obvious parallels with notions of 'centring' from other disciplines). In listening to her client the counsellor is trying to *echo* the client's felt sense so that he can hear it. The client can reflect on the counsellor's words and how far they seem to resonate with

---

Box 3.5 The 'Flavour' of the Felt Sense

In this extract Donald, the client, has for some time been getting quite blocked in talking about his relationship with his wife. The counsellor moves him from thinking about his relationship in wide general terms to focusing on just one aspect of it: his imminent holiday with his wife. Focusing on this one small concrete element enables Donald to see the 'flavour' of his felt sense of the relationship with his wife.

DONALD: I suppose Helen and I get on OK really. We have achieved quite a lot in our marriage – and the kids seem happy enough people. Maybe we could do more together now that the kids are up and away from home.

COUNSELLOR: One thing you're going to do together is go on that holiday. I remember you said that this was going to be the first time that you have been on holiday together, alone, for more than twenty years. What do you feel when you reflect upon that holiday? . . . Maybe take a few moments just to focus on that.

DONALD: [pause] [Donald sits rigidly up in his seat] I feel . . . scared . . . terrified . . . it's horrible – it's like I'm going to choke . . . 'suffocate'. [Some minutes later]

DONALD: . . . of course it's not just about the holiday – it's just that that throws our relationship into sharp focus. It's really that I have no idea what our relationship is going to be like. It's so long since we have just been with each other. I am so scared that I'm going to find it suffocating – that all the restrictions we've built up while having the kids will still be there even though they aren't . . . that there will be nothing else left that's healthy.

---

his felt sense. Often it helps if the client re-states the words for himself; indeed it is interesting how often a client will actually say the words again for himself as though he were sounding them out to see if they resonated with his felt sense. Perhaps they do, or perhaps he can improve them. When the right handle-words have been found, their resonance with the felt sense is usually experienced by the client as a great release of tension. Indeed, often the client actually exhales deeply or expresses that relief in words. Gendlin also talks about *the body talking back*. This is relevant when there is a distinct lack of resonance between what the client is saying to himself and what his felt sense actually is. There was an illustration of this in Box 3.4 when the client paused, tried to contact his felt sense, but then said 'no – I am just excited'. These words clearly did not fit his felt sense, as was later evident. In saying this to himself it is likely that his body would have reacted to the lack of fit. Sometimes this is experienced as a sudden tension or just a powerful experience of wrongness. This 'talking-back' has many striking parallels. For instance, a similar kind of phenomenon sometimes happens to people when they have very important decisions to make. Often it is only when people actually make a decision that they realise just how important the other choice is to them. For instance, when a couple finally decide that they will definitely separate, that is often the very time when one or both of them realise that deep down they really want to be together. Sometimes people also report a similar kind of phenomenon when they have come closest to taking their own life. It is only when they have been at the very point of choosing to end their life that they have the clarity of sensing that they do not want that.

In this chapter we are concerned with the counsellor empathising with the client. Gendlin takes this a step further by teaching clients how to empathise with themselves. He calls this *focusing*. In focusing, the client is essentially applying client-centred attitudes and responses towards his felt sense. His felt sense is then 'the client's client' (Gendlin, 1984). There are many variations of the focusing technique and, far from demanding that people follow a rigid laid-down procedure, Gendlin appreciates the uniqueness of each client and each client's client by emphasising that people can develop and refine their own particular approaches.

FOCUSING ON THE THERAPEUTIC RELATIONSHIP

If the client can turn his empathic sensitivity inwards, then so too can the counsellor. This becomes an important part of supervision in the person-centred approach where the 'presenting of cases' does not put the same emphasis on the intricacies of the client's personality as would occur in other disciplines, but where much more attention is given to the counsellor's appraisal of the relationship between the client and herself. Box 3.6 reproduces a series of self-questions which help the counsellor to 'focus' on the therapeutic relationship and her part in it.

The authors' experience is that counsellors seldom reach the end of the questions in Box 3.6 without some new area for exploration being opened up. If the counsellor has been experiencing difficulty in work with a client, these kinds of questions, in helping the counsellor touch the edge of her awareness, often throw light on what has been causing her difficulty in relation to her client; for example: 'I realise that I've been going through the motions with him, but I've not really been willing to get *involved*' / 'I feel a stiffness when I think of him – I wonder if that comes over to him and what it has to do with in me?' / 'I thought that I could handle his racism, but I realise it has been getting to me' / 'I find her so attractive – so full of life – I suspect I may be making it difficult for her to show me her ugly side'.

Box 3.6 Focusing on the Therapeutic Relationship (An ingredient of person-centred case-study)

Who am I in our relationship?
Who does he see me as?
What does he most need from me?
What do I most want to give him?
When I consider him, what sensation do I experience – *Is that all?*
What are his beautiful bits?

(focusing on each of these in turn)

*What do I experience when
I focus on this? – Is that all?*
What are his ugly bits?

(focusing on each of these in turn)

*What do I experience when
I focus on this? – Is that all?*

In this process of focusing on herself the counsellor is using her sensitivity to uncover the many factors which may influence her ability to release that sensitivity in relationship with her client. In the next section we explore some of the factors which most often enhance or inhibit the counsellor's ability to release empathic sensitivity.

RELEASING EMPATHIC SENSITIVITY

Are empathic counsellors born or made? There are a variety of assumptions about the basis of our empathic ability. Some people assume that we are either born with it or not. If this assumption were true then much of counsellor training would be superfluous – all that would be needed would be a way of selecting those who 'had it'. An opposite assumption is that empathic ability is wholly learned. This puts the emphasis much more on training than selection, since it becomes possible to 'train' any person to be empathic.

The writers take a stance which is only slightly different from this second position; we see empathy as the counsellor's own *intellectual and emotional sensitivity focused on the client*. This sensitivity has been developed through many years of observing and relating with people in life's varied contexts. Even the three-year-old has already developed sufficient sensitivity to judge her parent's mood and reaction to small misdemeanours. By the time adulthood is reached this sensitivity to others has been built upon literally millions of interpersonal encounters. Each one of us has this immense reservoir of sensitivity which, potentially, we can focus upon our client. Hence the process becomes one of *releasing this sensitivity*. The effect of training should be to help the counsellor to release her sensitivity more often and more fully, as she requires. We regard this gradual release of sensitivity as a developmental process in the counsellor – a process which can be facilitated by trainers, supervisors and counselling experience, but one which is essentially under the control of the counsellor. In the early stages of this development the issue for the counsellor may be her *willingness* to take the step of empathising. It is much easier, and *safer*, to stay within one's own frame of reference and pronounce upon the client's situation. In so far as that procedure conforms precisely to the medical model the client may even expect and accept that level of un-involvement from the counsellor. But the potential person-centred counsellor is likely to be dissatisfied with such superficial contact, and more and more she will take risks with releasing her empathic sensitivity.

Research evidence consistently supports the finding that experienced counsellors offer a higher degree of empathy to their clients than less experienced counsellors (Barrett-Lennard, 1962; Fiedler, 1949; Mullen and Abeles, 1972). But as well as experience being a variable so too is the degree of 'integration' of the counsellor. At one extreme, personality disturbance and a lack of personal development in the counsellor correlate with lower empathic understanding, but even feelings of discomfort and a lack of confidence in relationships reduce the counsellor's empathic understanding (Bergin and Jasper, 1969; Selfridge and van der Kolk, 1976; Bergin and Solomon, 1970). This last finding is particularly interesting because it reminds us that empathy is not necessarily a static quality which we exhibit regardless of circumstances. The counsellor's ability to draw upon her sensitivity, and have confidence in it, is dependent on the relationship the counsellor has with the client and also on how 'centred' she is as a person. The counsellor 'empties herself' in order to 'receive' what is happening in the client, and it follows that whatever disturbs the 'stillness', sometimes called 'centredness', of the counsellor is likely to interfere with the release of her empathic sensitivity. Such factors are usually called *blocks to empathy*, a few of which are discussed in the following pages.

Perhaps the most surprising 'blocks' are the counsellor's own theories about human behaviour. (See also Mearns, 1997a: 129–132.) Any theory which she uses to predict individual human behaviour is a potential menace lying in wait to distract the counsellor from focusing her own highly developed sensitivity on the individual world of her client. Sometimes these theories have some basis in psychological research, for instance:

Depressed people can't think well.
Less intelligent people will be less able to verbalise their problems.
The client's anger or affection towards me will likely be signs of his 'transference'.

Other theories have no basis in research, but may be held just as strongly; often these might be called 'prejudices':

Rich people don't have 'real' problems.
Facing squarely up to difficulties is the most helpful way to progress.
Women will likely be more vulnerable than men.

Theories of either kind are useless for predicting the behaviour of an *individual* client. Even theories grounded in psychological research only reflect trends or averages in human behaviour: they cannot tell us how a particular client will feel or behave. Rather than be seduced by theories it is more productive to empathise with our client in order to discover his individual and unique responses. Perhaps this is one of the reasons why some psychologists find the person-centred approach so difficult. They have to lay aside so many of their riches, their theories of human behaviour, before they can experience the individuality of their client.

But we all have theories about human behaviour, and to some degree we will have an emotional investment in their fulfilment. We shall not only expect them to be correct, but at an emotional level we may *need* them to be correct. For this reason a major emphasis in person-centred training is the uncovering and challenging of personal theories. However, even when personal theories have become explicit, as Box 3.7 illustrates, they might still be a 'block' to the counsellor's understanding of an individual client.

Box 3.7 Personal Theories Can Get in the Way

A counsellor reports on her work with an earlier client:

I remember working with a recently 'separated' woman client. I kept waiting and expecting to see some element of sadness or loss or depression – but none came. I kept thinking that I saw hints of such emotions, but she denied these. So then I began to think that she must be blocking all these things, and I tried to help her to find ways through these blocks. I think she got pretty fed up with that. It was only after some weeks of distinctly inaccurate empathy that I realised that what was getting in the way was my personal theory on what recently separated people felt: that they would feel sad/ lost/depressed. It had been extremely difficult for me to see this lively cheery woman who wanted a little bit of assistance with restructuring a new set of elements in her life.

One particular kind of 'personal theory' can be so disruptive of empathy that it deserves separate mention. This theory might be stated thus: 'If I have been in the same kind of situation as my client, then my client will probably experience it in a similar way to myself.' Having had *common experiences* can often ease communication and make it easier to establish early trust between client and counsellor. To the extent that the experiences actually are similar, then empathy might also be assisted: the counsellor might make intelligent guesses as to what the client might be experiencing. However, the counsellor should also be aware that common experiences can sometimes prove a hindrance to counselling by actually making empathy more difficult. The danger is that the counsellor will begin to identify with the client's position. This might be called *'false empathy'* because it can look like empathy but in fact it is not. It is where the counsellor puts herself in the client's position and wrongly assumes that what *she* would feel in that position is what the client is in fact feeling.

By far the most pervasive and troublesome blocks to the counsellor's empathy are *her own needs and fears* in the therapeutic relationship. 'Troubled people can't empathise' is a saying which is often applied to clients but sometimes it describes the counsellor as well. For instance, the counsellor's empathy might be blocked by such things as a mind temporarily preoccupied with other emergencies, by embarrassment, or perhaps even by a fear of the client's pain. Strong feelings of sympathy or antipathy towards the client can be 'blocks' which make it difficult to stay in the troubled present of the client. Sometimes inexperienced counsellors are blocked by their need to see the client as 'improving in every session', or perhaps by a more generalised 'need to be helpful'. The main symptoms of this last disease are that every session will end on a positive note; pain will never quite be faced; and empathic journeys will only follow safe and usually ineffective routes.

Where the counsellor has strong needs to be *liked* or *needed* by her client, 'stuckness' is also likely to occur, and the fullness of the counsellor's empathic experience may be lost in competition with such forceful needs. In some such cases the counsellor is so linked through need with her client that she cannot be open to him changing because that changing might fundamentally affect herself. Every counselling approach recognises this dilemma as one of *over-involvement* (see Chapter 7). It is much more difficult to listen to someone whose change will affect oneself. One special case of this is in the counsellor's relationship with her partner. Often there is the implicit assumption that someone who spends her time listening to strangers should be able to do that particularly effectively with her partner, but of course that is not so easy, because we are somewhat 'involved' with our partner. Counsellors sometimes give themselves a hard time with that kind of expectation!

Releasing one's empathic sensitivity is an act of giving. The counsellor is giving herself as a mirror to the client. In one of the last articles before his death, Carl Rogers (1986d) reminded us of the importance of clarity in this mirror. He quotes from an earlier article by Sylvia Slack (1985), who commented thus on a counselling session with him:

> It was like Dr Rogers was a magical mirror. The process involved my sending rays toward that mirror. I looked into the mirror to get a glimpse of the reality that I am. If I had sensed the mirror was affected by the rays being received, the reflection would have seemed distorted and not to be trusted.

When the counsellor is troubled and therefore vulnerable she does not so readily give her empathy, and if she does it is likely to be distorted with her own turmoil. When one is vulnerable a normal response is to *defend*: not to open oneself through empathy, but to withdraw and keep the client at a distance. As counsellors develop through training, experience and supervision, it is to be hoped that they become sufficiently *self-accepting* so that they have less need to be defensive with clients. A part of the process of training and continued development as a person-centred counsellor is becoming aware of the personal factors which are likely to be blocks to skills such as empathy. Indeed, *personal development* is regarded as the fundamental dimension of training (Mearns, 1997a).

Concentrating as we have on the notion of blocks to the release of our empathic sensitivity is a rather negative way of looking at the counsellor's development. We might equally well have described that development in terms of 'blocks overcome', for as the counsellor grows in confidence and competence she becomes able to release her empathic sensitivity in a wider variety of ways. She can trust, and therefore use, more and more of herself in relationship with her client. As this development progresses the three basic interpersonal dimensions of empathy, congruence and unconditional positive regard become more integrated until they are as they should be – inseparable. In interaction the three dimensions reach their full potency. For instance, the perfect combination of empathy and congruence is best described by Jerry Bozarth (1984) with his notion of *idiosyncratic empathy reactions*. In essence this idea recognises that the way a counsellor would react empathically to what a client is experiencing would likely be quite individual to that counsellor. If the counsellor trusts herself she can give the client *whatever* her reaction is in that moment, in the knowledge that her own blocks are not distorting the reflection. Box 3.8 gives one example of an idiosyncratic empathy reaction. In the Box the counsellor had felt her empathic reaction to Jim welling up inside her. She was professional enough to know that this was her empathic sensitivity, and not 'false empathy', so she released it.

Box 3.8 An 'Idiosyncratic Empathy Reaction'

Jim, the client, has spent the first 30 minutes of this session describing how he has 'got his life together' six months after the death of his wife and child.

JIM: Things were difficult . . . really difficult . . . but having to look after the other two kids really helped. I mean I just had to be there for them – I couldn't just go AWOL. I had to be there for them. I always have to be there for them. They are all that matters . . . nothing else. I got 'down', but I could always fight my way out of it. I never missed a morning getting them up or an evening putting them to bed. Now I'm OK really – at first I wanted to look after them all myself, but now Jean [his mother-in-law] does as much as I do, and that's OK. Sometimes things get difficult at work – something happens and I feel the tears welling up in me – but I can usually force them away.

At this point Jim stops talking, because he notices that a tear is running down the counsellor's cheek.
A few seconds later Jim starts crying too.

For anyone who has a picture of empathy as represented by the counsellor nodding wisely and repeating the last six words the client has said, idiosyncratic empathy reactions might seem like a welcome breath of fresh air. Jerry Bozarth has indeed taken the lid off empathy by suggesting that the experienced counsellor might dare to trust her congruent reaction, *whatever that is.* His thesis is even more radically exemplified in a case study by one of the present authors (Thorne, 1987), and this whole issue of the coming together of empathy and congruence is further explored in Chapter 5 (see Box 5.2).

Just as empathy perfectly integrates with congruence, unconditional positive regard also takes its place as inseparable from the other two – inseparable, that is, except by writers who divide books into chapters!

NOTE

1 Liverpool and Everton are major English soccer teams who have a particular rivalry. At all soccer games rival sets of supporters are strictly segregated within the stadium. Being a 'Liverpool supporter at the Everton end' would represent extreme social isolation!

4

Unconditional Positive Regard

If it was difficult to restrict the process of empathy to specific behavioural responses, unconditional positive regard is just as elusive since it is an *attitude* of the counsellor. However, it is possible to define this attitude in fairly straightforward language.

> Unconditional positive regard is the label given to the fundamental attitude of the person-centred counsellor towards her client. The counsellor who holds this attitude deeply values the humanity of her client and is not deflected in that valuing by any particular client behaviours. The attitude manifests itself in the counsellor's consistent acceptance of and enduring warmth towards her client.

The distinctiveness of this attitude in the person-centred approach lies in its *consistency*. The person-centred counsellor is able to manifest the attitude with the whole range of clients regardless of how they behave. It is easy to value the client who works hard and shows a lasting respect for the helper but the attitude is more challenged where the client is repeatedly self-defeating, sees himself as worthless, actively manipulates other people to their detriment, or masks his vulnerability with direct aggression towards the helper.

This attitude of acceptance towards the client is not only consistent from client to client but is enduring throughout the person-centred counsellor's relationship with any one client. The client feels that the counsellor values him consistently throughout their relationship, despite the fact that he may not value himself and even if the counsellor does not like or approve of all the client's behaviour. It is possible to accept the client as a person of worth while still not liking some of the things he does. Often this basic acceptance will be severely tested by clients whose outward behaviour may at times be very unpleasant. Box 4.1 gives an example of one such client who was difficult to accept, but whose behaviour became understandable once the counsellor was able to make the step of acceptance.

Box 4.1 A Nothing Person who is Scared to Love

Mary was a teacher who came to the counsellor on the recommendation of a friend. Throughout the first interview she remained cold, somewhat aloof and not particularly enthusiastic about what counselling could offer her. She talked with relish about her hatred of schoolchildren:

> I hate the little ——s. They come in every day laughing at you. When you shout at them they snigger and go quiet for no more than a minute. To try to teach them French is pointless: all I try to do is teach them the rudiments of polite behaviour, albeit in French. Probably the only pleasure I get is making them squirm. Some of them are so cocky you shouldn't take them on, but you can do a good job on some of the little ones. I take great delight in making them cry.

Most people would be offended at the brutality of this teacher's attitude towards young children. A normal reaction would be to dismiss her attitude as unacceptable and endeavour to get her to rethink the morality of continuing in the profession. However, making such judgements is not the job of the counsellor, for these would merely close communication rather than deepen it. Accepting that this violent behaviour does not represent the whole of the human being helps the counsellor to stay interested, concerned and even warm towards her. In the third counselling session we find something which helps to make sense of this teacher's outward violence towards others when she says:

> I get so sad sometimes . . . so very sad. I never can show that to anyone. I just cry alone in my flat. I can be so horrible with people . . . it's just that I'm scared of them . . . I suppose I'm scared they'll see me . . . me as I really am . . . a nothing person who is scared to love.

There are many words used to describe this interpersonal dimension. Already we have referred to *unconditional positive regard* and *acceptance*. Another which was once widely used was *non-possessive warmth*, and *respect* has on occasions been a preferred label, although it does not in itself describe many of the essential features of the dimension: it is possible for instance to 'respect' someone quite coldly and conditionally. A word which Carl Rogers used to represent this dimension was *prizing*. In his American context this was a good choice since it communicated a greater intensity of feeling than most of the other terms. Similarly David Cain (1987) uses the word *affirming* to emphasise the function this attitude serves for the client: it 'affirms' his value. One word which is *not* an appropriate label for this dimension is 'liking'. This difference is important for trainees to whom the thought of 'liking' every client that comes through the door does not make sense. As is described elsewhere (Mearns, 1994: 3–5), 'liking' in our culture is a highly 'conditional' matter. We generally attribute our 'liking' to someone who shows similar or complementary values to our own. Our 'liking' is thus conditional on that similarity or complementarity. However, *valuing* the client as a person of worth is not conditional – it is equally possible to feel that deep valuing of the humanity of a person who displays a pattern of values quite different from our own. In that way, what our client generally experiences as the counsellor's 'liking' is, in fact, something much more loving and much more powerful – because it does not demand they meet our needs.

In this book we shall restrict ourselves to the use of the conventional label *unconditional positive regard*, with *acceptance* as a shorthand form, although it should be noted that in its literal sense it is impossible to achieve 'unconditional' positive regard. Every counsellor is human and fallible and therefore must have some 'personal limits' that might be exceeded by her client: the counsellor cannot therefore guarantee unconditionality. However, the person-centred counsellor is likely to be 'less conditional' than most other people with whom the client will relate. (See Purton, 1998, for a discussion of the spiritual implications of unconditional positive regard.)

Why is Unconditional Positive Regard Important?

The client who has been reared under oppressive 'conditions of worth' (see Chapter 1) will have learned that he has value only in so far as he behaves in accordance with the expectations of significant others. Unconditional positive regard on the part of the counsellor towards her client is important because it directly sabotages such conditions of worth: the counsellor values her client irrespective of the client's conforming to 'conditions'. Lietaer (1984) uses the term *counterconditioning* to describe the process set in motion by a counsellor's unconditional positive regard: the conditioned link between meeting conditions of worth and being valued is broken by continually treating the client as valuable in his own right, regardless of whether he meets the conditions of worth set out for him in his life.

In sabotaging conditions of worth, unconditional positive regard breaks into the client's negative, self-defeating cycle (see Figure 4.1).

The client who is lacking self-acceptance behaves in a way which reflects that attitude: he does not expect people to value him, so in relation to

FIGURE 4.1 *Self-defeating cycle*

others he is self-protective or *defensive*. He may appear weak, inappropriately aggressive, unemotional, or perhaps he tends to withdraw from intense social contact. Behaviours such as these are scarcely welcoming for other people, and may indeed drive them away, a fact which offers further evidence to the client that he is unloved and unlovable. Unconditional positive regard breaks into this cycle as the counsellor refuses to be deflected by the client's defensive behaviour and instead offers the client consistent acceptance of his intrinsic worth.

This different behaviour of the counsellor has effects on the client's behaviour in the relationship. Since there is now no need for the client to be defensive in relationship with the counsellor, his fear gradually reduces to create the kind of trusting environment where he feels safe enough to explore previously fearful domains.

As well as having influence through contradicting conditions of worth and helping the client to feel less defensive, the counsellor's unconditional positive regard has a much more direct impact upon the client's valuing of himself. In a sense the client becomes 'contaminated' by the counsellor's attitude and little by little he begins to experience the same attitude towards himself. It is only when the client begins, however tentatively, to value himself in this way that real movement can take place, and in the case of so many clients this first self-valuing is the direct outcome of sensing the counsellor's valuing of them and accepting that such an attitude is possible.

That her attitude of unconditional positive regard can eventually have such a dramatic effect is something which the person-centred counsellor must remember early in the therapeutic encounter when the client may come armoured with protective layers and bristling with defences which have been serving the purpose of keeping other people away.

SOME 'DEFENSIVE' CLIENTS

Sometimes it is hard work for the counsellor not to be put off by this outward *defensiveness* of their client. For instance, Mary, Roger and James are clients who had evolved their individual ways of defending themselves and preventing intimacy in relationships.

Mary was 45 years old and didn't look after herself. Her hair was unwashed, her clothes were old and a mixture of black and grey. Her face was drawn and relatively expressionless despite the intensity of feeling which was underlying her appearance. She also smelled. She sobbed during most of the first two sessions and ended both with the sentence 'I don't know why you would want to bother with the likes of me.'

Roger, 35 years old, was a successful businessman who came reluctantly to counselling with his wife. In the first session he spoke about his wife being the cause of their problem because 'she doesn't know her place'. In Roger's opinion new friends of his wife were 'filling her head with a lot of fancy ideas'. Roger's solution to their problem was that 'if she would just return to being a proper wife then everything would be OK'. Speaking about his work, Roger talked with relish about a small competitor whom he had recently put out of business through granting a loan which he knew could not be repaid in the allotted time. 'It was less costly to take a loss on his loan, then buy up the bankrupt business for a song, rather than to buy him out as a going concern.' Roger thought that his former competitor was a 'wimp' for attempting suicide after the affair.

James was 18 years old and difficult to work with because he was alienated, suspicious and angry. The following extract occurred 30 minutes into the first counselling interview. Much of the preceding time had been taken up with James taunting the counsellor: asking her if she had any training, why she was 'so very old', and laughing at the clothes she wore. The counsellor had not found the 30 minutes easy by any means, but had been intent upon outlasting James's barrage. As time went by, James escalated his attack until he climaxed it with:

JAMES: Okay – you tell me how I should get a job . . . go on . . . tell me. . . 'advise' me that's your job after all . . . go on . . . earn your money, you charlatan!'

COUNSELLOR [*after a long pause*]: It feels like you're trying to push me more and more . . . like you really want to fight or something like that.

JAMES: Yes. You're right I want to fight – you're just like all the rest . . . a do-gooder who's only in it for herself. I bet you like to think of yourself as 'a good person who helps people'. Well I think you are a ——. I think you're no good – go on earn your money, you bitch.

COUNSELLOR [*after a long silence*]: I do feel hurt . . . I feel sad as well [*silence*] what do you feel? . . . do you feel hurt as well? [*Long silence*]

As it later transpired, these three clients had four things in common:

1 they were all deeply sad,
2 they all felt intensely unloved,
3 they did not love themselves,
4 they were all highly vulnerable.

The behaviour of these clients looked quite different because their vulnerability showed itself through different defensive patterns. Mary withdrew into her deeply hurt 'child', while Roger projected unfeeling arrogance and superiority and James used anger, suspicion, alienation and outright aggression as his way of keeping people away. Their defensiveness repelled other people because as a shield to the outer world it hid who they really were as people. Unconditional positive regard involves not being deflected by the defensive shield but waiting, continuing to value the worth of the person and thereby *earning the right* to be allowed behind the shield.

'PERSONAL LANGUAGES'

The particular way in which an individual defends his vulnerability is just one aspect of his *'personal language'*: his characteristic ways of expressing the various facets of his self. If the counsellor was working with a client from a different culture, and with a different language, she would probably be particularly patient, tolerant and concerned to discover the meaning of his language. She would be wary of forming early judgements, because she would know that those judgements might simply be based on her lack of understanding of his language and culture. For the counsellor who is trying to develop her attitude of unconditional positive regard it can be helpful to make the same kind of assumptions about *all* her clients. She might start by assuming that each new client has his own 'personal language' which he will use to express himself. The counsellor's task, principally through empathy, is to uncover and understand that language. This is a useful approach for the beginning counsellor because it helps her to stay focused on her client, rather than be deflected by any of his behaviours. Instead of becoming judgemental about his behaviour the counsellor is concentrating on the question *what does this behaviour mean for this client?* Here are a few examples of aspects of 'personal languages' with their individual meanings for the clients concerned.

Jim's jokes usually mean that he is tense.

Polly's tears often mean that she is angry.

Robert's anger often means that he is sad.

Sally's effervescence usually means that she needs to be admired.

That smile from Peter means that he is hurting.

Jane's 'crying for the world' is her being in touch with her 'soft' part which she values enormously.

A tender word from Gus is a strong message of love.

Sid's obsession and precision with words reflects his genuine desire not to hurt others through misunderstanding.

Bert's brusque directness reflects his fear of manipulation.

Mick's repeated lateness probably means that he is uneasy with what is happening.

Doug's repeated lateness probably means that he likes to feel that he is in control.

Charlie's repeated lateness means that he is sloppy about timekeeping.

As the counsellor gradually learns the personal language of her client his behaviour becomes more intelligible and the person behind the behaviour becomes progressively easier to see and to accept. In a similar vein the psychoanalytically trained Bruno Bettelheim referred to the task of working with severely disturbed children as one of 'discovering and understanding the logic upon which the child's behaviour is based' (Bettelheim, 1987).

BUT WHAT DO I DO WHEN I JUST DON'T ACCEPT MY CLIENT?

Later in this chapter we shall go into more detail on the personal work which the counsellor can do to develop the attitude of unconditional positive regard, but an early concern which inexperienced practitioners might have is what practical steps they can take when faced with their non-acceptance of a client.

Usually this problem arises early rather than later in a counselling relationship; it may be that the counsellor instantly dislikes the client, or as early as in the first or second session feels herself withdrawing a little from the relationship. When the counsellor senses such withdrawal one practical step she can take is to pay much more attention to *empathising* with the client. This effort might not come easily when her instincts are to withdraw, and she may have to reinforce her efforts by repeatedly remind-ing herself of the fact that '*I don't know this person yet*'. This conscious move into empathy can have two beneficial consequences: firstly, it shifts the counsellor's attention from herself to her client, and secondly, the empathic process itself can help to disclose new facets and depths to the client which may bring the counsellor's early judgement into question (as in Box 4.1).

The next practical step the counsellor can take is to attend to herself in supervision. With the help of her supervisor she might address the ques-tion: 'What do I *not* know about this client?' This can be a useful question because it not only opens up new areas for possible exploration, but it reminds the counsellor of the limited evidence on which her early judge-ment is based. Attending to this question might be supplemented by the exercise: '*focusing on the therapeutic relationship*' which was presented in Chapter 3 (Box 3.6). Hopefully explorations such as these will help the counsellor to find the key in herself to the source of her judgement. Underlying these practical steps which the counsellor can take is the acknowledgement that the counsellor's dislike is indeed *hers*, and therefore her responsibility. It is not sufficient for the person-centred practitioner repeatedly to project responsibility for her feelings on to her client.

We started this section by assuming that most cases of non-acceptance would occur early in the counselling contact, but there are, of course, instances where difficulties arise later in the therapeutic relationship. If the counsellor does not attend to these difficulties they can lead to her gradual withdrawal from the relationship and a consequent 'stuckness' in the therapeutic process (see Chapter 7). Once again the counsellor may attend to these problems in supervision, but she may also openly explore such difficulties with the client so that they can both be involved in their resolution. This procedure not only helps the development of their rela-tionship, but will often uncover important therapeutic material for the client. Examples of the counsellor being congruent about difficulties such as these are given in Chapters 5 and 7 and in the exploration of the '*unspo-ken relationship*' between counsellor and client (Mearns, 1994: 64–74).

CAN THE CLIENT ACCEPT MY ACCEPTANCE?

Most often the client is relieved to find that his counsellor seems to value him and has not been repelled by the difficult things he may have said or done. Clients may even voice their relief at the end of a first session and comment on how good it feels to be attended to in this way. However, sometimes a client has had such a history of rejection that this is what he expects from the counsellor. In extreme cases the client seems to be so ready for rejection that he actually encourages it: 'I can't see what you see in me – I'm really no good, you know!' A danger for the inexperienced counsellor is that she is drawn into the client's self-fulfilling expectations and actually becomes increasingly judgemental towards her client. One counsellor reflected upon this during supervision on her work with a client called Andrew:

> I realise that as time has gone on I have come to dread appointments with Andrew. He is just so negative that it has drawn me into also becoming negative with him. In recent times I have been increasingly stern with him and have made far too many suggestions as to how he might change his life. I bet I've become more and more cold with him too. For his part I think this has let him retreat more and more into his 'rejected little boy'.

If a client has a long history of not being accepted, he may initially distrust the counsellor's acceptance. His life may have been a catalogue of people offering different forms of love and then withdrawing the offer, so why should he trust it this time? Such a client may reserve judgement on the counsellor's acceptance, and in some cases the client may even present the counsellor with a series of 'tests' of her acceptance; if the counsellor negotiates these hurdles then the client may be prepared to trust (see Lambers, 1994d: 119). Exactly the same testing of the helper's acceptance is noted by people from other traditions working, for instance, with children from emotionally deprived backgrounds (Bettelheim, 1987; Neill, 1960). Box 4.2 reproduces the reflection of one client who had had difficulty in trusting the counsellor's acceptance.

A particularly difficult situation for any counsellor is where the client does not accept the counsellor's unconditional positive regard on the same basis as it is offered, but sees the counsellor's warmth as offering the possibility of an intimate relationship beyond the counselling setting. One of the many issues involved for the counsellor in such a situation is to communicate her limits clearly, while at the same time continuing to show her acceptance of the client. An over-reaction by the inexperienced counsellor might be to withdraw some of her acceptance lest it continue to be misinterpreted. If she did this she might find that she was unwittingly repeating a pattern of rejection which had often occurred in the client's life. It is not easy to be clear about limits while at the same time also communicating valuing. There can be no stereotyped way of handling such a delicate situation, but Box 4.3 reproduces one such example.

Box 4.2 Acceptance Can Be Difficult to Accept

Near the end of their time together a counsellor and client may devote some time to reviewing their counselling process (see Chapter 8). The following extract is taken from one such session, where the client is reflecting on the ways in which she had tried to dismiss the counsellor's acceptance.

> At first I had a lot of difficulty with the fact that you thought I was OK as a person – that you even seemed to 'like me'. That was so strange for me that I didn't believe it at first – nobody had ever liked me – including me! When I realised that you weren't pretending – that you really *did* like me – I began to think that *I* was the one who had been pretending – I must have been pretending to be OK as a person, otherwise you couldn't possibly like me. The next explanation I came up with was that if I really showed you all my horrible bits then you couldn't possibly like me – so I proceeded to show you me as I saw myself – the lowest of the low. It was only when I found that even this didn't put you off that I realised that *I could be all of me* with you and that wouldn't be destructive to either of us.

FOCUS ON WARMTH

Research is clear on the fact that simply *feeling* accepting towards the client is not enough, that acceptance has to be *communicated*. For one counsellor a genuine, spontaneous smile will be a means of communicating, while others will show their warmth by using words or physical contact. Each counsellor will likely have her own particular *repertoire* – her own characteristic ways of showing warmth. One aspect of developing as a person-centred counsellor is the expansion of one's repertoire so that warmth can be shown in different ways with different clients. For some clients verbal messages of warmth are not trusted, or perhaps are not trusted as much as, for instance, touching, but on the other hand there are

Box 4.3 Accepting the Client who Loves You

This extract is taken from near the end of a fairly lengthy counselling contract. The counsellor had tentatively raised the issue of termination since it seemed to her that the work had been substantially done and the contract might well be terminated with provision made for future reviews. During most of the session they had been discussing this possibility, although all the time it felt as though the client was coming to something special. A fairly long monologue from her climaxed with:

CLIENT: . . . so I realised that what I've been feeling really for the first time in my life, is how much I love someone. I guess it's pretty inconvenient that that someone happens to be you . . . but it's true. I realise that that's why I've been hanging on – I've dreaded the thought of ending. I don't really *need* you anymore, but it's difficult . . .

COUNSELLOR: . . . difficult to let me go?

CLIENT: Yes – I know it's the right thing to do . . . but it's difficult . . .

COUNSELLOR: I feel that at this moment you are trusting me with something very very precious . . . something very tender and delicate . . . a very beautiful gift . . .

CLIENT: . . . it feels like all of that to me too.

COUNSELLOR: Scared I might damage it?

CLIENT: No . . . not really . . . I don't think I would have given it to you if I had feared that.
[*Silence.*]

COUNSELLOR: What are you thinking?

CLIENT: I'm thinking that it's OK for us to end now.

clients for whom touching represents an assault. Box 4.4 lists a number of ways in which counsellors communicate their warmth. This list is by no means complete but it can be useful to help the counsellor to reflect upon her own repertoire.

Warmth helps to develop trust within the counselling relationship. Too little warmth will slow the development of trust and the process of counselling. There will also be some cases where too great a show of warmth, however genuinely felt by the counsellor, may be difficult for particular clients. These cases will be quite rare and confined to clients who are particularly suspicious of warmth from other people. In such instances it

Box 4.4 Ways of Communicating Warmth

Each individual counsellor will have her own repertoire of ways of communicating warmth. It is interesting to reflect on how easy or difficult it might be to use each of the following:

> going to the door to meet the client,
> shaking hands with the client,
> using the client's first name,
> smiling,
> using a 'warm' tone of voice,
> holding eye contact,
> genuinely laughing as the client recounts a funny incident,
> agreeing to extend the session where that is possible and
>   appropriate,
> using words to show warmth,
> showing genuine interest in the client,
> physically moving towards the client,
> touching the client's arm,
> touching the client's shoulder,
> holding hands,
> hugging the client.

would be a mistake for the counsellor to stop showing warmth for that would simply repeat the cycle of rejection mentioned earlier. Instead the counsellor would continue to show warmth but perhaps could use other, less intrusive, methods from her repertoire.

'Touching' is a natural and literal reaching out of one human being towards another, but many workers in some cultures find it enormously difficult to show their warmth through touch. The problem with touch is circular: when there is not much touching in a culture it begins to take on a mysterious connotation and hence it is mistrusted and little used. Yet when touching occurs in counselling it usually is experienced as perfectly natural and not at all discontinuous with the flow of communication between those involved.

For some counsellors the use of touch comes easily, while for others it is quite slow to develop. The difficulty centres on *trusting one's touching*; knowing when touching is our genuine felt response to our client rather than an imposition of our own need. As the counsellor explores her own use of touch, she might uncover instances where her touching is imposing, and she will learn to recognise those signs. An example of 'imposing' touching might be found in the amateur helper whose hugging of her client is not an expression of her warmth and willingness to stay with her client's feelings, but instead is saying something like 'there there now – stop this crying . . . because I can't stand it!'

Since the first edition of this book eleven years ago we need to acknowledge that the counselling culture has changed more in relation to 'touching' than to any other dimension of counsellor behaviour.

The problem with touching is that it is a powerful expression. That power may be expressed and experienced as caring. It may also be expressed and experienced as abusive. Just as in any other profession, some counsellors abuse their power and touching often plays a part in sexual abuse.

Other professions, further down the road of 'institutionalisation' (Mearns, 1997b), note similar re-positioning with respect to physical contact. The primary school teacher who, in 1988, might have sat the hurting pupil on her lap and given her a cuddle, would be advised by her union and her management to maintain strict non-contact in 1999. The social worker who regarded seriously the position of having a child 'in care' might have offered an appropriate parental 'holding' in 1988, but would maintain her 'professional' distance in 1999. Rightly, we have become concerned with abuse and weekly we are alerted to examples from ten, twenty and thirty years ago when abusers worked themselves into situations where they could meet their exploitative needs in the knowledge that professions did not have safeguards.

As two men in a profession where clients are often vulnerable and men are more often the abusers, we feel this dilemma painfully. Both of us have struggled in our own ways with this dilemma, and we have also offered each other enormous support. There is no easy answer – indeed our personal distress over this matter is best expressed by the conclusion, 'there is no answer in a sick society'.

Yet, we continue to believe that person-centred counselling is an endeavour which is grounded in our humanity and if we are to withdraw dimensions of our humanity from the work we would be offering a charade to our clients and to ourselves. So we will not restrain our gentle touch on the hand or shoulder – a touch which arises spontaneously out of our sense of being in 'contact' with the other human being. Nor will we restrain our sincere offer of a hug when we genuinely want to offer that and when our client wants to receive it. We *will* be respectful of our client in these instances and we will take care to appreciate his experiencing. But we refuse to withdraw our humanity from our work and an essential part of our humanity is that we are embodied.

The danger in our writing these words is that *others* will take them as licence for their own abusiveness. There is no way out of this dilemma. It may eventually silence us as writers or finish us as counsellors but at least we shall have retained our integrity.

FOCUS ON CONDITIONALITY

Early in this chapter we asserted that most liking in everyday life is *conditional*. Implicit in any relationship is a whole set of 'conditions' which could complete the sentences: 'I will like you more if you . . .', and 'I will not like you so much if you . . .'. Even in very close relationships much of the liking of one person for the other could still be conditional on the other 'not changing too much' or 'continuing to love me' or any number of other specific conditions.

Counselling is *not* everyday life, and unconditional positive regard is not the same as our conditional 'liking'. The challenge for the person-centred counsellor is to enhance her own security, stability and self-acceptance so that she has less need to meet others in the kind of self-protective fashion which engenders conditionality. A great deal of the emphasis in person-centred training is focused on this dimension of the counsellor's self-acceptance.

A first step for the counsellor would be to become aware of the different kinds of situations in which she is likely to find difficulty with conditionality. Box 4.5 reproduces 26 situations which have been used in voluntary sector training with couple counsellors to help them to explore the conditionality of their liking (Mearns, 1985).

An exploration such as that in Box 4.5 can begin the process of clarifying the counsellor's values, because it is when values are contravened or threatened that the counsellor is more likely to become conditional in her valuing of the client. Awareness of her values, and the effect these are likely to have on her acceptance, can in itself give the counsellor some measure of control. Furthermore, awareness of values also gives the counsellor the opportunity to question the basis of such values and explore them further. Sometimes the counsellor might find that the value has very little basis in her actual experience but is something she has introjected from parents, and serves no important function for her in the present. However, at other times the counsellor will find that the value which is being challenged has a firm foundation in her own psychology. It may for instance be rooted in her own needs and fears. Accepting the client relatively unconditionally might thus be particularly difficult and threatening for the counsellor. The most obvious example of this is where the client does not value the counsellor; can the counsellor continue to value him despite this or must she retreat to defend her self-esteem?

Box 4.5 How Conditional is my Liking?

In an exercise to explore conditionality, couple counsellors were faced with this list of 26 situations and asked to reflect on how easy or difficult it might be for them to accept such clients:

A husband who questions your competence as a counsellor.

A husband who says, 'My wife promised to obey me and that is what she must do; there is nothing further to discuss.'

A feminist who has come to dislike men in general, including her husband .

A woman who says: 'I want to leave him because he's boring and I've found someone younger.'

A client who swears continuously.

A client who talks non-stop, but never about his feelings.

A drug pusher who works the primary schools ('elementary schools', in the USA).

A miner who talks about 'breaking heads' on the picket line.

A heroin addict.

An Evangelical Christian who always seems to be trying to convert you.

A father who has battered his baby.

A male client who discloses that he's gay.

A couple who tell you: 'You haven't helped us a bit, and if nothing happens in this session we may as well stop.'

A woman who feels that the husband should make all the important decisions in a relationship.

A husband who lets his wife do all the talking and gives you that look which says 'What right do you have to pry into my life?'

A couple who repeatedly accuse you of not telling them the solution to their problem.

A policeman who talks about 'breaking heads' on the picket line.

A young man who has mugged an old woman.

Box 4.5 continued

A woman client who tells you that she is a lesbian.

A client who never seems to change.

A woman who accepts that being beaten regularly is a normal part of married life.

A husband who regularly batters his wife.

A client who complains about his life but doesn't even seem to be trying to change.

A mother who has battered her baby.

A client who tells you that he is in love with you.

A client who tells you that she is in love with you.

Supervision as well as training in the person-centred approach involves continuing attention to the counsellor's personal development and is concerned with uncovering and understanding basic needs and fears in the counsellor which might channel her into conditionality. Box 4.6 illustrates a trainee counsellor's discovery of personal needs which had inhibited her work. In this case the needs were related to her valuing of the person-centred approach: the counsellor discovered that her acceptance of clients was to some extent 'conditional' upon them following person-centred values.

Sometimes the counsellor's needs and fears are related to the institutional setting in which she is working. Institutions are more often 'institution-centred' than person-centred, and their clients are seldom accepted unconditionally Hence the counsellor in an institution might actually be open to criticism if she is *not* conditional. For instance, the school counsellor may be criticised by colleagues for valuing the disruptive pupil, or the clinical psychologist might find difficulty with psychiatric staff who see her acceptance of a 'manipulative' patient as 'naive'. Such pressures as these would be rightly feared by the person-centred counsellor, because loss of credibility in the eyes of colleagues is a severe sanction. It would not be surprising if the counsellor became more conditional with her clients, and in that way reflected the conditionality of her institution.

Uncovering and facing our own needs and fears is of course part of the therapeutic process which is associated with developing self-acceptance (see Chapter 2). Where the counsellor accepts herself she is not so easily

Box 4.6 Can the Person-Centred Approach Accept its Opposite?

In the following extract a trainee counsellor speaks with her supervisor on her development over the past year and in particular on two significant hurdles which she has negotiated:

> Critical issues for me this year have been firstly to realise how unaccepting I had been towards clients who only seemed to want to talk about their thoughts rather than explore their feelings. Of course, I was so convinced by the importance of feelings that I felt that every client had to go there right away – it was just one of the things that the person-centred approach would take so much for granted, that I kept pushing my clients down that road and was decidedly unaccepting of their resistance. The other hurdle, although it was related, was more difficult to overcome: I found it very difficult to accept one client who seemed intent on moving in a direction which clearly seemed to be opposite to that of growth . . . It's like all my work with clients was at some fundamental level conditional upon them moving in the direction of growth . . . conditional upon them confirming the person-centred hypothesis. I had great difficulty with this one client who seemed intent on going back to her husband for regular beatings. I could be open to her thoughts about leaving him but every time she talked about going back I would 'get her to reflect on it more deeply'. The poor woman soon realised that she could only give me that part of herself which was wanting to leave her husband; meanwhile the other part which wanted to return to the marriage remained unexamined, mysterious and even more compelling. It was through that client that I realised that the person-centred approach was even more challenging than I had ever thought, because to be really person-centred you actually have to value the client who may be moving in a direction opposite to growth – opposite to everything you value.

or profoundly threatened by her client. This makes it easier for her to be free in the counselling setting; free to use her warmth in whatever ways are meaningful, free to enter the most scary parts of her client's world through empathy and free to respond at all times to her client in ways which are perfectly congruent with how she feels. We now turn to this third, and perhaps most challenging freedom of all – *congruence*.

5

CONGRUENCE

Box 5.1 Can I Dare to be Me?

In response to my client, can I dare to:

Feel the feelings that are within me?
Hold my client when I feel he needs to be held?
Show my anger when that is strongly felt?
Admit my distraction when challenged about it?
Admit my confusion when that persists?
Voice my irritation when that grows?
Put words to my affection when that is there?
Shout when something is seething inside me?
Be spontaneous even though I do not know where that will lead?
Be forceful as well as gentle?
Be gentle as well as forceful?
Use my sensuous self in relation to my client?
Step out from behind my 'professional facade'?

Can I dare to be *me* in response to my client?

Congruence poses challenging questions like those in Box 5.1, but its challenge only exists because helpers generally support a norm of incongruence. Indeed, perhaps we should be dismayed at the level of incongruence we find in mental health provision. Can it make sense to work with clients and patients who struggle with their incongruence by offering them our own incongruent relating? The fact that this question is not seriously asked in mental health provision needs to be addressed from a sociological perspective. Incongruent relating is so thoroughly ingrained within our culture that it has become viewed as the healthy reality. As human beings we use our considerable skills to cultivate our incongruence such that we are protected from being openly 'seen' by the other. As is described elsewhere, we create *'lace curtains* and *safety screens'* (Mearns, 1996; 1997a) to hide from others and, in collusion with others, we develop *'restrictive norms'* to ensure that in our relating we minimise the possibility of meeting each other freely (Mearns, 1994: 67–8). If we were able to free ourselves enough from the cultural norm of incongruence we might be able to question our stance – we might even be able to consider our culture in terms of its 'collective pathology of incongruence'.

We defined empathy as a 'process', unconditional positive regard as an 'attitude' and now we define congruence as a 'state of being' of the counsellor in relation to her client:

> Congruence is the state of being of the counsellor when her outward responses to her client consistently match the inner feelings and sensations which she has in relation to the client.

The counsellor is 'congruent' when she is openly being what she *is* in response to her client – when the way she is behaving is perfectly reflective of what she is feeling inside – when her response to her client is what she feels and is not a pretence or a defence.

On the other hand when she pretends to be 'clever' or 'competent' or 'caring' she is being false in relation to her client – her outward behaviour is not congruent with what is going on inside her. Moustakas (1959: 201) talked about the importance of his congruence in psychotherapeutic work with children:

> I saw that I must stop playing the role of the professional therapist and allow my potentials, talents and skills, my total experience as a human being to blend naturally into the relationship with the child and whenever humanly possible to meet him as a whole person.

For congruence to have an impact on the relationship between counsellor and client the latter must *perceive* the counsellor as being congruent. It does not matter how authentic the counsellor is being: if the client perceives her as duplicitous or insincere the therapeutic impact of congruence will be substantially lost. At times the counsellor must work very hard to be believed, particularly by the client who has had considerable experience of *incongruent* helpers.

Like unconditional positive regard, congruence has several names in common usage, one of which is 'genuineness'. This can be confusing to new students since in everyday language the word 'genuineness' usually implies some conscious control; that is to say a person can *choose* whether to be genuine or not. However, as we shall see later in this chapter, incongruence on the part of the counsellor is not necessarily a deliberate withholding; alternatively it can arise from the counsellor's lack of self-awareness in regard to her feelings towards the client.

Other alternative terms are 'realness' and 'authenticity'. These have the advantage of describing how the client often experiences this dimension: *'She* [the counsellor] *behaves like a real person – she seems really authentic in the way she relates to me'.* One disadvantage of these terms is that they beg the question of what is *authentic* or *real*: is the counsellor ceasing to be *real* when she is behaving defensively and hiding her responses? The word *congruent* has the advantage of emphasising that what is being described is the contiguity between the counsellor's underlying feelings and her outward behaviour. However, even this most used term can occasionally cause difficulty to the new student who confuses it with the notion of 'congruence between two people'. The student might take the statement: *'the counsellor was perfectly congruent with the client'* to mean *'the counsellor was perfectly in tune with the client'*, hence early confusion between congruence and empathy can arise.

WHAT DOES CONGRUENCE LOOK LIKE?

Congruence is a state of being of the counsellor throughout her contact with the client, and as such it usually goes on unnoticed. When it is noticed that may be because it radically changes the direction of the therapeutic process, or perhaps it is distinctive because the counsellor's words, superficially at least, do not seem to fit with what is expected of a helper. Let us look at a few examples of congruent responses which stand out from their background while remembering that 95 per cent of the counsellor's congruent responding will go unnoticed.

Sample 1

The client has been speaking for some time on how he is going to leave his wife when suddenly he stops and asks the counsellor if she is following him; does she understand? To this the counsellor replies:

> No . . . in all honesty I *don't* understand . . . you're talking about leaving your wife . . . but for some reason I'm not understanding very well . . . [*long silence*] it's like you've got it all thought out in a very complex step-by-step way . . . and it's *so* complicated . . . but I don't at all understand where your *feelings* are in all this.

Helpers sometimes feel uneasy about admitting that they are not understanding the client: perhaps they assume that their lack of understanding is an indicator of inadequacy. In the above example the counsellor was not defensive about her difficulty with understanding. She was open about that lack of understanding, focused on it in herself and realised that one of the things which was making it difficult was that although her client had many thoughts about his situation he had not been so clear about his feelings. The counsellor's congruent response proved to be important since the client was indeed unsure about his feelings.

Sample 2

This sample is taken from the middle of the ninth session with the client, Andy. Following the previous meeting the counsellor had reflected in her notes upon her growing irritation in relation to Andy. The persistence of this feeling led her to comment upon it when it recurred in session nine:

> It's strange – quite often in recent sessions I've been feeling uncomfortable – kind of irritated, and impatient. I'm not sure what's behind it, but it's that kind of persistent feeling which is often quite useful . . . It feels . . . Yes, it feels like I'm getting more and more constrained . . . restricted – that maybe our relationship isn't as fluid as it used to be. How does it feel to you?

It later transpired that this congruent response helped the counsellor and client to break out of a rather dangerous pattern which had been developing in their relationship. This pattern involved Andy becoming increasingly dependent upon the counsellor, and the counsellor taking on that more dominant role which culminated in her recurring discomfort. The counsellor was curious about this response to her client, and although she did not immediately understand it, she felt it was such a persistent response on her part that it was likely to be relevant to the client and their relationship, so she was open about her own confusion. The counsellor and client were then able to discuss their reactions to each other and map out the way they had slipped into this dominant-submissive pattern. In the next session Andy talked at length about his realisation that in his relationship with his wife the pattern which had gradually evolved was one where, in any stressful situation, his wife would take on the 'dominant' role while he slipped into the complementary 'submissive' way of being with which he was no longer satisfied. The counsellor's willingness to be open about her own difficulties in relationship with the client had helped Andy to become aware of his part in this pattern. This is highly characteristic of the person-centred approach, where the relationship formed between counsellor and client is a real one from which learnings can be made and generalised to other aspects of the client's life.

Sample 3

This sample is taken 30 minutes into the first session with the client, Bob. Bob has spent most of this time telling his story: he has had experience of the whole gamut of psychiatric services including four periods of hospitalisation for a total of three years; two courses of electroconvulsive therapy; more or less permanent usage of minor tranquillisers, as well as some periods on major tranquillisers and in his own words 'some group therapy'. The lack of affect in his description suggested that he had told his story many times before. When he had finished, he looked the counsellor straight in the eye (for the first time) and said: 'Do you really think you can help me?' To this the counsellor replied slowly and uneasily:

> [*Long silence*] . . . No . . . no . . . I can't see how I can help you . . .
> [*pause*] it feels like you're so tied up by all that past experience that it's
> difficult to know who you are, never mind knowing whether or not I
> can help you.

This may seem a very risky thing for a counsellor to say in a first session with a client: indeed for the counsellor who is developing her use of congruence, it *feels* very risky. In this case the counsellor's congruent response proved important for two reasons. Firstly it was a great relief to Bob to find a helper who did not promise to help him: every other helper he had met had promised that – and none had succeeded. The content of the counsellor's congruent statement was also useful to Bob; he realised that it was indeed difficult to know *who* he was. Later in that session he reflected on the fact that he had come to think of himself as his psychiatric history: as though he was nothing else but his psychiatric history. For the first time in many years he began to explore what else he was.

In this sample the counsellor gave her genuine response to the client even though this at first seemed to run counter to what helpers 'should' say. Of course, the counsellor was doing more than just giving this reaction and leaving it at that; she was staying attentive and responsible to the consequences of her reaction. This responsibility which accompanies congruence is more dramatically illustrated in Sample 4, below.

In the above samples it is easy to see how the counsellor's congruence was actually helpful to the client, but it would be grossly misleading to suggest that this is always the case. There are times when the counsellor's reaction may be strongly felt but not particularly helpful to the client at that moment. When this happens the counsellor's responsibility to the client and their relationship becomes particularly important. Rather than withdraw and wait to explore the event in supervision, the person-centred counsellor would show more responsibility to her client by remaining open and congruent about her apparently unhelpful behaviour. The counsellor has a responsibility to be *fully* present in the relationship with her client; that means not withholding important events in order to consider these in the relative safety of supervision. The following sample not only illustrates the fact that the counsellor was drawn into a judgemental position but also that, after a silence which permitted a change of content, she was able to reflect congruently upon her own behaviour.

Sample 4

This 19-year-old client, Pete, had been showing considerable progress over previous sessions, but since the last meeting he has been rejected by a new girlfriend. This seems to have thrown him back into his former feelings of inadequacy:

> PETE: So once again I've got ditched . . . she didn't want me either . . .
> I've lost again – *failed* again . . . she's *gone* just like all the rest . . . I
> don't blame her . . . it's not her fault.
> COUNSELLOR: I know – it's *you* – 'poor you' – rejected again – like

always! . . . [*pause*] I'm sorry, that was sarcastic of me . . . I was taking a 'dig' at you – Oh! [*shaking herself vigorously*] I got really wound up at what you were saying – it sounded so hopeless, so inevitable, so self-defeating . . . and it happens again and again and again. It's like I wanted to shake you and say 'Don't be such a wimp – You don't need to sink into self-pity – You can be more than that!'

PETE: But it's not my fault!

COUNSELLOR: Then whose is it [*in a raised voice*]?!

PETE: OK, it's my fault [*head bows – looks sullen*].

[*Silence.*]

COUNSELLOR [*speaking slowly*]: I feel pretty bad about myself 'battering' you like that. I don't think that was very clever of me and I don't think that it was very helpful of me. I think I reacted so strongly because I really do care about you – and was so frustrated that once again, after it looked like you had gained so much, when one thing went wrong you slipped right down again. I guess I'd got a bit too desperate on your behalf, and that made it difficult for me to listen to you and really understand how this is for you. How *do* you feel?

PETE: [*Pause*] I feel frustrated too – I'm annoyed with myself too – I'm more annoyed with myself than you are! I can't believe that I've dropped into 'poor me' again when one thing goes wrong. That's why this is such a big thing for me – not because of the girl – but because maybe I haven't changed as much as I thought I had.

In Sample 4 the counsellor would not have been very proud of the first half of the interaction where she has twice found herself reinforcing Pete's pattern of self-deprecation by adding her own criticism. '*Don't be such a wimp*' and '*Then whose is it?!*' Such flashes of annoyance would not be regarded as a therapeutic use of congruence; the counsellor has got over-involved (see Chapter 8) and is simply venting her frustration on the client without regard to the possible usefulness of her response. Counsellors make mistakes like this, but fortunately in our sample the counsellor shows responsibility to her client and recovers the situation by being fully congruent in her third and final statement. Sometimes a congruent response is short and intense, but at other times it is lengthy, with the counsellor trying to describe as accurately as possible the fullness of her response to the client. For instance, in the counsellor's final statement in Sample 4 she offers an array of feelings and thoughts: 'I feel bad' / 'not very clever of me' / 'not very helpful of me' / 'I really do care' / 'I was frustrated' / 'I got desperate' / 'difficult for me to listen and understand'. This full response, which shows all that she is experiencing, gives a context to her earlier behaviour and, hopefully, makes it understandable to the client. Indeed, her full response does more than recover the situation: it moves the process forward because it helps Pete to become aware that his own disappointment about not having changed is a large part of his present reaction.

As well as being aware of all the thoughts and feelings which comprise her congruent response to her client, the counsellor would have learned how to describe her feelings accurately. The most important ingredient in this is that she represents her feelings for what they are – *her* feelings. It is *her* anger, boredom, affection, desperation, etc. In everyday living people often project responsibility for their feelings on to other people: 'he makes me feel bored', 'she is a boring person' / 'she makes me angry' / 'she makes me feel sad', etc. Yet another way in which counselling is different from everyday life is that the counsellor has learned to take responsibility for her own feelings and she represents them to the client in similar fashion: 'I am feeling bored' / 'I am angry' etc. This accuracy in representing feelings can make it easier for the client to listen through difficult confrontations because the presentation is less accusatory. Furthermore, it shows the client that it is possible for people to take responsibility even for difficult feelings.

Before person-centred counselling begins to look like an arrangement whereby the counsellor can indulge herself in venting all her feelings while getting paid for the privilege, we must examine some guidelines which might be helpful to the less experienced counsellor.

GUIDELINES FOR CONGRUENCE

Our working definition at the start of this chapter looked clear and simple. It suggested that for congruence to be in existence the counsellor's outward responses to her client should consistently match her inner experiencing in relation to the client. For a more complete understanding we have to explore in detail the kind of counsellor experiencing which is implied, because plainly not all the counsellor's sensations are appropriate to the counselling contract. The counsellor cannot simply express whatever she is feeling in the moment (as in the first part of Sample 4) on the grounds that she is 'being congruent', else the counselling session would become more focused upon her than on the client. It is necessary to pre-scribe three guidelines which would generally govern the counsellor's therapeutic use of congruence.

First, when we talk about congruence we are referring to the counsel-lor's *response* to the client's experiencing. The counsellor may have lots of feelings and sensations flowing within her but it is only those which are in response to her client which are appropriate for expression. In this regard it is important to note that congruence is not the same as self-disclosure; congruence does not imply that the counsellor is open about herself and her life. Such self-disclosure, sometimes called 'willingness to be known', is a contentious issue in counselling. Barrett-Lennard (1962) hypothe-sised that the counsellor's willingness to be known would be significantly related to therapeutic outcome, but that hypothesis did not prove to be statistically significant. Our own view is that clients differ on this matter; for some, the counsellor's self-disclosure is a relevant dimension in that it helps the client to trust. For other clients, however, it is equally obvious that the last thing they want to do is to listen to the counsellor's experi-ence! In any case it is important to distinguish between self-disclosure and congruence. When the counsellor is being congruent she is giving her gen-uinely felt response to the client's experience at that time. Only rarely would this response disclose elements of the counsellor's life, and even then the focus of attention would remain on the client rather than the counsellor. For instance, the counsellor might say:

> I remember when I lost a close loved one – I also felt that kind of 'desolation' which you've described, but you are saying something more . . . you are saying that as well as feeling desolation, you are feeling . . . a kind of . . . annihilation?

A second guideline for a congruent response is that it must be one which is *relevant* to the immediate concern of the client. Sometimes the response which the counsellor has towards the client's experience is only really rel-evant to the counsellor herself. For instance, the client talking about his marriage might lead the counsellor to think about the marriage of another client; or the client talking about his stress might lead the coun-sellor to reflect upon the phenomenon of stress in general. Although these experiences of the counsellor are in response to the issues which the client has brought, the counsellor would not normally interrupt the client's flow to express them, because it is unlikely that they will be relevant to the client's experiencing.

In a counselling session the counsellor may experience a catalogue of responses to her client. Even if she were only to respond to those which were relevant to the present concerns of the client, the counsellor might still dominate the session. Hence a third guideline becomes necessary: that the feelings which the counsellor responds to tend to be those which are *persistent* or particularly *striking*. The counsellor would not do anything about a mild feeling of irritation that drifted in and out of her awareness, or a brief flash of annoyance in relation to one particular thing which the client said. But if that irritation or annoyance persistently recurred, or was so striking that it was important to the relationship between counsellor and client, then perhaps it might require attention. In Samples 1 and 3 the counsellor was responding to striking feelings of confusion and impotence, while Sample 2 found her expressing her persistent feeling of discomfort. In Sample 4 the counsellor's congruence in the second half is an effort to retrieve any damage which had been caused by her earlier flashes of annoyance and sarcasm.

In identifying 'persistent' as a guideline we also need to draw attention to the danger of the counsellor hiding behind this and slipping into the phenomenon which we call 'splurging congruence'. This depicts a pattern where the counsellor is customarily incongruent with her client over long periods of time then discharges all that pent-up unexpressed feeling in one large lump of projective material. The splurging may be done in the name of 'being congruent', but the motivation is generally punitive and is certainly experienced that way. This counsellor needs help with her chronic incongruence and her judgementalism.

In summary, then, it is necessary to qualify our working definition of congruence lest it is presumed that the counsellor should give expression to every fleeting sensation which she experiences during the counselling session. When we talk about being 'congruent' we are referring to the counsellor giving expression to *responses* which she has which are *relevant* to her client and which are relatively *persistent* or *striking*. These guidelines may appear to rule out a lot of what is conscious for the counsellor, but in fact they usually include most of the important material.

Even then these are only 'guidelines' for the less experienced practitioner who might otherwise struggle with the question of the appropriateness of her reactions to the client. As she gains experience and understanding of herself she will become fluent in her congruence and able to trust her instantaneous judgement of appropriateness. At this stage in her development the counsellor is able to be fully present and use herself in the therapeutic relationship. Her congruence will not be obvious because it is the norm: instead incongruence will stand out as different, and indicative of difficulties. Indeed, looking at examples of incongruence can be very helpful for the counsellor's understanding of the nature of congruence.

SAMPLES OF INCONGRUENCE

Most cases of incongruence are not as glaring as the examples which follow. In supervision, incongruence may be identified after examining the whole taped interview or even a series of interviews: only then is the gradual change in the counsellor observable. For instance, it may be that the counsellor is slowly becoming less spontaneous and more guarded. No single piece of the interview stands out as incongruent but gradually the counsellor is detaching herself from the relationship. This 'creeping incongruence' is very difficult for the counsellor to notice without help through supervision and analysis of tape-recordings of her work. Occasionally incongruence is more glaring; for instance, there is the 'double-message' where the counsellor is trying to hide her true response; her words may say one thing, but her non-verbal expression says another. Such a case would be the counsellor who says: 'I think it would be good for us to meet again as soon as possible', while simultaneously looking bored! Other common examples include the counsellor's warmth which is so effusive that it takes on an air of unreality, or that irritatingly regular 'mm-hm' which pretends that the counsellor is listening when in fact she may not be.

Counsellors will have developed numerous ways of being incongruent because incongruence is so ingrained in our culture. One of the reasons why person-centred training places more emphasis on group work than individual therapy for personal development is that it is more difficult to sustain incongruent forms of relating in groups, at least in groups where there is a norm of confrontation (Mearns, 1997a).

Samples 5 and 6 report two glaringly incongruent responses reproduced verbatim, and with some embarrassment, from tape-recordings of sessions.

Sample 5

CLIENT: I don't think you like me.
COUNSELLOR: Of course I like you.
   [*Silence*]

93

In this example the counsellor was perfectly aware of the fact that she did not like the client very much, but she lied. It is never easy for a client to challenge the counsellor, and that was certainly true in this particular case. It had been a tremendous opportunity for the counsellor to respond to the fact that her client was willing to invest so much in the relationship that he could even look at its difficulties. Unfortunately the counsellor could not take that opportunity by providing a congruent response and a comprehensive follow-up to that response.

Sample 6

CLIENT: You seem angry with me today.
COUNSELLOR: No, I'm not angry . . . it's just that I've had a lot on my plate today.
[*Silence*]

The reader will have guessed that the counsellor *was* angry. However, in this particular case her incongruence was due to a lack of awareness of that anger within her. There seemed to be no lasting damage from her incongruence, only temporary confusion in the client who was, of course, quite clear that the counsellor was angry. In between sessions the counsellor realised her incongruence and made a point of dealing with that at a later opportune moment.

These samples illustrate two quite distinct forms of incongruence which can occur at the points A and B in Figure 5.1.

Incongruence A is where the counsellor has underlying feelings in response to the client, but is *unaware* of these and hence does not give expression to them. Sample 6 exemplifies this form of incongruence. Incongruence B is

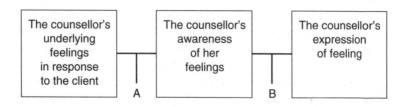

FIGURE 5.1 *Two forms of incongruence*

where the counsellor is aware of her feelings but *chooses* not to give expression to these (e.g. Sample 5).

Another example might help to clarify the difference between A and B. In incongruence A, the counsellor might have mounting feelings of irritation or impatience, but because she is not aware of these she cannot respond to them. Although the counsellor does not notice her own incongruence, her client might sense that something is wrong as he perceives changes in the counsellor's non-verbal behaviour. He may feel the counsellor's tension or perceive her tone of voice becoming more cold and detached. He may notice the counsellor avoiding eye contact or sense the loss of quality in the interest she is showing. In incongruence B the same result can arise, but for a quite different reason. Here the counsellor would be aware of her mounting feelings of irritation or impatience, but she may resist giving expression to these feelings even though they are persistent and relevant responses to the client. Again her client may be sensing the discontinuity between the counsellor's experience and expression. The client does not know what the counsellor is doing but his own sensitivity leads him to be suspicious.

This difference between incongruence A and B was shrewdly alluded to by one particularly perceptive client who, after repeated incongruence on the part of his counsellor, faced her with the question: '*Who are you trying to fool, ma'am: me or you?*' If she was trying to fool *him* then it was incongruence B, but if she was fooling *herself* it was incongruence A!

In exploring reasons for counsellor incongruence it is again important to distinguish types A and B. Incongruence A can be related to the counsellor's lack of self-awareness, or it may be that she has personal difficulties in the area to which the client is attending. For instance, a counsellor who fears anger might find that her incongruence increases as that issue is approached by her client. Alternatively the incongruence may mirror the position of the counsellor in the relationship. For example she may be unaware of her growing alienation or detachment in relation to the client, but these would still lead to a deterioration in the quality of her presence and consequent incongruence.

The bases for incongruence B, where the counsellor is consciously withholding, can be similar or quite different. Perhaps the counsellor is able to give expression to 'nice' feelings, but not to 'bad' feelings, and in a few cases the exact opposite may be the case. Alternatively the counsellor may be too tired, emotionally or professionally, to be fully present and so she prefers to go through the motions of a helping interview rather than actually get involved in it. At other times the counsellor may be protecting some image of herself in the client's eyes; for instance endeavouring to have the client see her as *expert, powerful,* or *coherent and stable.* Protecting such myths about the power of the counsellor might help to engage the faith-healing dimension of helping but does not have much to do with being congruent. In some cases incongruence B, like A, may be related to other emotions within the counsellor; for instance *fear*. One of the present authors writes about this elsewhere:

> I am aware that my incongruence B has a lot to do with *fear*. When I protect my client from my authentic response I am in fact protecting *me* from the possible consequences of my feelings. It is nice and easy to say 'that would be too difficult for my client to take right now' or 'perhaps I'll work that out a bit more in my head and then talk it out with her – it might be too confusing the way it is just now'. These are nice reasons for not responding to my client, but they can just as easily be rationalisations. Underlying them can be things like 'she might be horrified at me saying that' / 'he might stop liking me if I said that' / 'I don't know what would happen next if I said that'. Such fears inhibit congruence. For that matter, fear can also inhibit empathy and unconditional positive regard. (Mearns, 1986: 8)

Having explored some specific examples of congruence and incongruence we need to emphasise that these give a misleading picture of the phenomenon. These were introduced as striking, somewhat discontinuous responses. The examples of congruence only represent a tiny proportion of the counsellor's congruent responding. The majority takes the form of the counsellor being experienced by the client as fully 'present' with him – being willingly attentive and genuinely interested in him with no hint of wanting him to be different from that which he is expressing. It is the wholeness and consistency in that quality of presence (Mearns, 1994: 5–8; Thorne, 1997c: 209–10) which properly depicts the counsellor's congruence more than how she handles a small percentage of testing incidents.

Why is Congruence Important?

Like empathy and unconditional positive regard, congruence makes it easier for the client to *trust* the counsellor and the counselling process. If the client accepts the counsellor as congruent then he will know that the response he gets from her can be accepted as open and honest. He knows that the counsellor is not concerned with manipulating him and consequently he can feel more free in their relationship. One counsellor in training used a phrase which captures this ingredient. In writing about the importance of the counsellor's congruence she observed that: 'being present gives presence to the other' (McDermott, 1986). In the person-centred approach congruence dissolves the mysteriousness of the counsellor. Mystery evokes the illusion of power; transparency dissolves it. Trust clearly can exist in relationships where the counsellor is mysterious and hidden, but it is very much the kind of trust one would have of a being who is regarded as superior. In the person-centred approach the aim is to establish a more egalitarian relationship where the counsellor *earns* trust rather than *commands* it through mystery and superiority. The trust which the congruent counsellor earns is that of a person who is willing to be fully present as a real, alive, relating human being who is not concealing.

A second, but related, way in which congruence can be important occurs through the counsellor's willingness to be open about *weaknesses*. She is open to being confused, powerless, mistaken, and apologetic, when these are parts of her congruent response to her client. This openness about apparent weaknesses can introduce whole new possibilities for self-acceptance in the client who spends his life in fear of weaknesses in himself. As one client commented:

> It blew my mind when she [the counsellor] admitted that she hadn't
> been really understanding me – I mean she was serious, and apologetic,
> and yet still solid. If I had been her, that kind of thing would just have
> destroyed me. That was the moment when I first realised that it was
> *possible* for someone to have imperfections but still be OK.

A third reason for the importance of counsellor congruence relates to the very goal of counselling where, implicitly at least, *the client is endeavouring to become more congruent himself.* The client seeks to become more able to represent his feelings and responses in a straightforward, accurate way rather than hiding or disguising them. While 'modelling' is not a direct aim of person-centred counselling, it would be quite inappropriate for the counsellor to portray something *opposite* to the desired therapeutic outcome: it would indeed be impertinent for a counsellor to expect to further her client's congruence by being incongruent herself.

The fourth, and certainly the most important, benefit of congruence is one that has largely been ignored in the literature to date. Congruence is significant because it *enhances the quality of the response which the counsellor gives to the client.* In being consistently congruent the counsellor is offering to the client a reflection of the effects which the client's behaviour has on another human being whose integrity can be trusted, and whose professionalism has ensured that as far as possible that reflection is not discoloured by the counsellor's own need system. This is a powerful therapeutic phenomenon: the counsellor is not simply nodding knowingly and commenting wisely on the client's behaviour, but she is responding as a vibrant and trustworthy human being – it is little wonder that her congruent reactions can be potent in helping the client to move on.

The person-centred approach is often characterised as mild and unchallenging, but nothing could be further from the truth: the challenge of the counsellor's congruence is vibrant with possibilities. Certainly, in the person-centred approach that challenge is always in the context of the support provided by the counsellor's unconditional positive regard which offers the client a fundamental acceptance of his value. In that context, where the client feels valued, it becomes much easier for him to accept the challenge of congruent empathy in the counsellor. Samples 1, 2 and 3 illustrated the fact that the counsellor's congruent response could change the pattern of events and help both client and counsellor to see things which were not apparent before. For instance, in Sample 1 the counsellor knew that she did not understand the client and it was through her openness about that difficulty in understanding that both of them were able to discover the fact that the client was focusing almost exclusively on his thoughts rather than his feelings. In Sample 2 the counsellor's congruence about her discomfort in their relationship helped the client to see the submissive role created for himself in relationships. In Sample 3 the counsellor's congruence about the fact that she did not feel optimistic about being able to help the client allowed both to move to the realisation that the client had totally submerged his identity in his psychiatric history.

The person-centred counsellor gradually comes to trust the power and integrity of her congruence. There are times when she has absolutely no idea where her congruent response is going to take the client, herself, and their relationship. In that moment the two people are encountering each other in the full sense of that word. The counsellor has developed a kind of 'faith in her own process' which permits her to trust her own genuine response to the clients, and in that way use herself fully as a healing agent in the therapeutic process (see Thorne, 1987 and 1997a: 159 for striking examples of this). This is the central dynamic in person-centred counselling. In the same way that the psychoanalytic practitioner becomes familiar with transference and her own counter-transference, the person-centred counsellor fosters her own understanding of herself and her congruence. The totality of the person-centred counsellor's investment of self in the therapeutic relationship may be encapsulated in the case note reproduced in Box 5.2.

How Can the Counsellor Foster
her Congruence?

Trainee counsellors come to the person-centred approach with at least the rudiments of the attitude of unconditional positive regard and early in training it is common to pay particular attention towards helping the trainee to release her empathic sensitivity, but the therapeutic condition which is usually slowest to develop is congruence. Anything which has considerable power carries a proportionate threat of danger; the person-centred counsellor investing her *self* in the therapeutic process is full of power and danger and the trainee is wise to be cautious.

Essentially the danger implicit in congruence is that the counsellor's own needs and fears might become too intimately tied to her awareness of her client and hence confuse her congruent responses in a way that cannot be clarified by counsellor and client. *'But I was only being congruent!'* is a weak excuse for the counsellor who has imposed her own needs and fears on to her client. The freedom offered by congruence carries particular responsibilities for the counsellor's continuing self-development because it is through development that her own needs and fears become less imposing in the therapeutic arena (see Box 5.3).

The counsellors in Box 5.3 were aware of the influence in these examples of their own needs and fears. Learning in the person-centred approach involves the counsellor discovering and exploring aspects of her needs and fears which impose themselves in the counselling setting.[1]

As this work progresses the counsellor becomes more trusting of herself; learning to be congruent is inseparably linked with learning to trust oneself. If the counsellor is to use herself, including her congruent reactions, in the counselling relationship, then she must trust that self and those reactions. Usually she will not know where her reactions are leading nor even, in that moment, from where they are coming, but she will have learned to recognise the difference between a reaction which is probably

Box 5.2 Who Needs Words?

This case note was written by one of the authors (Mearns) after a session with Bob, a war veteran whose psychological damage had rendered him mute.

Tonight Bob and I had our most powerful session to date. When I went into his room he had 'American Pie' playing on the record player. As usual he was lying, fully dressed, on his bed. I sat precisely where I had finished the day before which was just close enough to touch him. Before I had come to him I had spent some time in the car, getting myself relaxed and centred. That was important because right away he looked into my eyes. His look was so fundamental – right away it shook my very being, but I was centred enough to meet it and to return it. He kept looking at me and I kept receiving it and sending back my own warmth. I lost track of time, as always, but it must have been about half an hour later because we had turned the record back to the 'A' side when I found myself crying, inside. I could feel it so strong – I was really choked and yet not a sound came out of my mouth. Everything flashed before me – I knew that my history had some similarities with his. But I also knew that I wasn't crying for *me* – my experience had been similar, but it wasn't with me then. It wasn't *me* crying – it was more *like he was crying inside me*. And that crying was so very very strong – and *mute*. As I looked at him and he looked at me it felt like love passed between us, from one to the other. I remember 'Vincent' was playing. I reached out to Bob with both my hands, and he put one of his between them. It was as though the touch had 'earthed' all the sensing that was so strong within us. I cried. Not that gentle tear that often is a response to the sadness in a client, but a deep deep sobbing. I remember being amazed at the strength of this feeling within me, yet, at another level, I knew that it was OK. Slowly, Bob cried too, and eventually his sobbing became screaming. He reached out and held me so tight [I later found that my back was bleeding from cuts made by his nails]. He let his desperation and his fear meet the light of our day. And I cried with him more and more.

As I write this note some hours later I know that we have begun. I also am aware that I am still trembling.

Box 5.3 Congruence Does Not Mean Imposing One's Own Needs and Fears

These two statements are from supervision sessions with counsellors in the process of discovering the ways in which their own needs and fears impose themselves in their counselling.

A   I wanted to just go over to her [the client] and give her a big squeeze – but I realised that that was my need to say 'there, there now, don't cry – I'll look after you – you poor little girl'. Squeezes can sometimes be 'giving' but sometimes they are 'taking away'. In this case it would have been keeping her as the little girl whom I can handle – and taking away the woman whom I find more difficult.

B   I feel so *angry* towards him – it is strong, it is persistent, and yet it is just not appropriate for the simple reason that it has absolutely nothing to do with him – it is my own horror of being partner to a man like him who treats his wife like furniture. I can't see his loving, his softness, or his fear, while I am blocked by my own fear.

---

empathic and one which is likely to stem more from her own needs or fears. In learning to trust herself she will have found that even her spontaneous reactions do not seek to destroy, and more often than not they prove to be helpful to the client.

This kind of discovery cannot be made by the counsellor simply reflecting on herself even with the help of the most able supervisor. It can only be achieved through the counsellor 'experimenting' with herself in real helping contexts, including counselling. New counsellors may feel uncomfortable with this idea of the counsellor experimenting, but in fact if the counsellor is to develop and change as a helper, then experimenting, in the sense of using different aspects of herself, is inevitably involved. Box 5.4 reproduces a counsellor's report of one example of experimentation. In this box the counsellor uses the phrase '*I forced myself to let it happen*'. This is a perfect way to describe the idea of experimentation with one's congruence. The counsellor had gradually grown to trust herself more, including her touching, but an important step in the process was to begin to let that happen in practice. Paradoxically, it often takes some deliberate intent to '*let it happen*'.

Such experiments are important steps in the counsellor's fostering of her congruence. In the example from Box 5.4 the counsellor has gained

Box 5.4 A Touching Experiment

This extract is taken from a trainee counsellor's 'personal profile' which is a journal focused on the personal development aspect of counselling training.

> Yesterday Ben [a client] was shaking and strained in his grief and I really wanted to reach out to him and put my hand on his. So often in the past I would have got lost in thought about how appropriate that may be, but this time I just forced myself to let it happen. As soon as I touched him it was as though some of my warmth went over to him and his tension released – he gasped and exploded in sobbing.

further confirmation that her congruent response was to be trusted. She has found one more aspect of her being which she can trust and use with clients.

In the process of fostering her congruence the counsellor will uncover more dimensions of herself which she can use constructively in counselling. These discoveries are exciting because the developing counsellor moves from a position where she invests very little of herself, often looking somewhat stiff and stereotyped, to one where she becomes progressively more free until it seems that almost every part of her being might be used in her work.

Fostering her congruence may be one of the later processes to which the trainee counsellor attends, but it carries an enormous dividend, not just for her clients but for the counsellor herself. Being congruent in counselling relationships is usually experienced by counsellors as *energising* rather than draining. Even if workers have not experienced this, they may recall its opposite: that working in a context where incongruence prevails is exhausting and debilitating.

As the counsellor gradually uses more of herself in her work her client is offered a vibrant, experiencing human being who combines an acceptance of him with an ability to step into his world and move around in it without fear. It is little wonder that this combination is powerful.

THE THREE CONDITIONS IN COMBINATION
AND CONFLICT

In Chapter 4 we have already discussed the relationship between empathy and unconditional positive regard, seeing these as related in so far as the existence of one facilitates the establishment of the other. In Chapter 3 we pointed to the perfect combination of empathy and congruence described by Bozarth (1984) as 'idiosyncratic empathy reactions'. In the present chapter we have developed this link between congruence and empathy by suggesting that the main function of congruence is that it allows the counsellor to be an accurate rather than a shadowy and distorting reflector to the client. We could go further with this combination of empathy and congruence by regarding much of the counsellor's congruence as the product of her *attending to her own felt sense in relation to the client* in that moment and giving the product of that attention to the client. Gendlin (1970: 549) spoke of this similarity between empathy and congruence:

> Congruence . . . means responding from out of our own ongoing experiential process, showing the steps of thought and feeling we go through, responding not stiltedly or artificially, but out of our felt being . . . As experiential processes, empathy and congruence are exactly the same thing, the direct expression of what we are now going through with the client, in response to him.

Unconditional positive regard and congruence are also related, with the existence of one facilitating the development of the other: when the counsellor accepts the client then it is easier for her to trust the client and feel free to use herself in a fully congruent way. Indeed, where counsellors experience difficulties with congruence in relation to a particular client, their person-centred supervisor will often invite them to consider how far they accept the client, since a lack of congruence can be a symptom of difficulties with trust and acceptance.

Being congruent can sometimes help to promote acceptance. This is referred to as '*taking risks in the relationship*': for instance, the counsellor may be open about a difficulty she has in relation to the client and if the pair can explore and clarify that difficulty then their relationship and mutual acceptance are often enhanced in exactly the same way as occurs in any relationship.

Probably the most frequent challenge to the person-centred approach

103

can be encapsulated by the question: '*What happens when your uncondi-tional positive regard and congruence are in conflict – are you congruent about your lack of acceptance?*' Carl Rogers was often asked this question, but rarely satisfied questioners, no matter what answer he provided! Part of the problem with this question is that the questioner and the experienced person-centred practitioner endeavouring to respond are gen-erally coming from quite different frames of reference. The questioner can readily imagine many contexts where she would experience that conflict, but the reality for the experienced person-centred counsellor is that this conflict simply does not arise. This may sound presumptuous in the extreme, but please bear with us. The developed person-centred counsel-lor does not have the kind of difficulty in valuing the client that is anticipated by the questioner. We have problems in valuing the other person when we are deeply threatened by the position adopted by that person. But the major thrust of the person-centred counsellor's personal development, over many years, has been such that they are less vulnerable within their own self – they are simply not threatened by the different value positions adopted by clients. They can consider the questioner's proposition theoretically, but it is simply not an issue in practice.

Nevertheless, we still need to consider this question for the developing person-centred counsellor. What does she do when she is confronted by a client who represents what she most fears? Should she endeavour to 'por-tray' some degree of valuing in the face of such a challenge? Actually, she might be able to do that because humans are so skilled at incongruence that they can be actors – a skill which is not observed in any other species. Should she, instead, immediately stop working with this client? Compared to the first option, this is an honourable choice, particularly if the coun-sellor *owns* her difficulty in the process and does not seek to project that on to the client. The third possibility is that the counsellor does not dis-connect with the client, but openly acknowledges her distress.

This is a difficult choice and it is not one which trainers should seek to force upon trainees because, in making this choice, the trainee is actually opting, in that moment, to work beyond her personal limits. It is different for the experienced practitioner who has developed some 'faith in the process' and can enter these uncertain situations with that accumulated credit. Nevertheless, it can be an important step for the trainee when she honours her own inadequacy over her skills at portrayal and is honest with her client despite her own fear. One early trainee counsellor con-tributed a report of that kind of experience, which we reproduce in Box 5.5.

Box 5.5 Being Honest

I got to the point where I couldn't continue with Jan [the client]. She was so openly lesbian that it challenged me in every session. I didn't know what to do with that – I was scared. I couldn't 'pretend' with her – she would see through that. I talked with my supervisor about terminating with her. Looking back on it, I realise that I talked that out with my supervisor so that I wouldn't do it. In the end what I did was to 'come clean' with Jan. I made a 'speech' one day. I took a deep breath and said that I was scared of her; I knew this was more to do with me than her; I didn't want to 'put it on her'; but I always had had difficulty with her expressed affection for me and that I hadn't been honest about that up to this moment.

Jan's reaction to my honesty took my breath away. She thanked me for my honesty. She said that she was both sad and angry at my fear of her. But, that it would have been much worse if I hadn't been honest. In that moment I remember wishing that I did not have this homophobic raft of fear within me, because I knew that, although we had been honest with each other, I could not go further with Jan until I had gone further with myself.

Congruence demystifies the counsellor's work because it shows simply and clearly what she is experiencing in response to the client. It shows that she is not harbouring complicated and threatening interpretations or theories about the client's pathology. It takes away the secrecy of counselling and ensures that the counsellor and the client share the same reality. Although therapeutic work with more profoundly disturbed clients is not the concern of this book it is worth noting that, in the opinion of these writers, congruence as a therapeutic condition becomes more critical with psychotic clients.[2] Where such clients find it difficult to share others' conceptions of reality, then it becomes of paramount importance that the counsellor gives the client a clear picture of her part of that external reality. Concealing responses, substituting these with other responses, or hiding behind techniques, send contradictory and confused messages to a client who is having enough difficulty in stabilising his view of the world. All too commonly, the human element in mental health care is *reduced* rather than increased with the more severely disturbed client to a point where he is actually kept away from other human beings through hospitalisation and even locked wards. Treatments also decrease in their personal element, with more emphasis being put on the impersonal processes of chemotherapy, and behaviour-shaping approaches rather than resourcing and researching the *consistent* use of the highly personal activity of counselling. The emphasis here is on the word 'consistent', because counselling work with the profoundly disturbed client can be different in that a considerable amount of the therapeutic time is spent earning his trust and helping him to feel safe (see Lambers, 1994a, b, c, d). Bruno Bettelheim (1987) noted in his work with severely disturbed children that their behaviour can at first become more disruptive as they test the trustworthiness of the humanity which is being offered to them: to work in a counselling way with the severely disturbed takes considerable commitment on the part the individual counsellor and also the employing institution.

Congruence is so basic to healthy human relationships and the development of trust that we must question any helping which minimises it. It is the professional responsibility of the counsellor to be fully present for her client, because her incongruence could certainly be *damaging* to someone who is already vulnerable. Early in this chapter we posed a question that might now be re-worded: '*Can I dare NOT to be me in response to my client?*' We close this chapter with Box 5.6, which gives one client's view on the importance of his counsellor's congruence.

Box 5.6 Can I Dare *Not* To Be Me in my Response to my Client?

Sometime after completion of counselling a client reflects back on his counsellor:

> She was always *there* – always alive – always present. At the beginning I didn't trust her – like I didn't trust she was sincere – that she would *stay* interested in me. No-one had ever stayed interested in me. It took a long time before I trusted her. But every time we met she was so trustworthy – so real. She would get pissed off at me and she'd say so – and it was OK. Sometimes I'd get pissed off at her and that was OK too – like people do get fed up with each other from time to time – that's the way things are, isn't it?

In exploring the intricacies of empathy, unconditional positive regard and congruence we have drawn examples from many points in the therapeutic process. It remains necessary to work through that process, systematically highlighting the issues which arise at different times. The logical place to commence such a journey is at its 'beginnings'.

NOTES

1 The reader who is familiar with the psychoanalytic concepts of transference and countertransference will realise that this section might easily translate into that language. It is common for different approaches to meet the same phenomena but conceptualise and emphasise them differently.

2 This opinion is supported by the Wisconsin study of person-centred therapy with schizophrenic patients. Those patients who perceived a high degree of congruence in their therapist were independently rated as showing the greatest degree of change. Furthermore, those patients who were in relationships where the therapist exhibited low congruence showed no change or even *regressive* change (Rogers et al., 1967: 86).

6

'BEGINNINGS'

THE POWER GAME

Most of us at one time or other have been humiliated by our reception at the hands of someone from whom we are seeking help or information. The classically traumatic situation is one where we are kept waiting in an inhospitable room full of out-of-date magazines and are summoned – half an hour behind schedule – by a disembodied voice through an intercom which tells us to go to the second room on the right. We follow the directions and arrive in front of a closed door. We knock timidly and receive no response. We knock again and an irritable voice bids us enter. We go in to be confronted by a figure at a desk writing on a note-pad. We are ignored for a further minute and then a face looks up and an arm waves us towards an uncomfortable chair in front of the desk. By now we are so seriously intimidated that we can scarcely recall why we have come.

The process we have just described may seem an extreme example but it demonstrates in a stark form the abuse of power which is disturbingly prevalent in some quarters of the helping professions. For the person-centred counsellor it is a matter of supreme concern that she does not unwittingly fall into a similar trap. For her, as we saw in Chapter 1, her actions and attitudes are desirably determined by a belief that it is important to reject the pursuit of authority or control over others and to seek to share power (see Box 1.9). The implications of this belief for the reception of and initial encounter with clients are considerable. They have a bearing on every aspect not only of the interaction between counsellor and client but also of the environment in which counselling takes place. Power games can be played with tables and chairs as much as with words and tones of voice. It is salutary for the counsellor to ask herself the question: 'What process does a client have to go through to get to me, and what messages does he receive along the way?' Box 6.1 summarises some of the questions which such an examination might raise.

THE CLIENT ARRIVES WITH HIS EXPECTATIONS

The counsellor who is awaiting a new client may well have difficulty in maintaining an openness to the experience of the first encounter. There can be many reasons for this but prior information often presents a major obstacle. Such information may be of the most limited kind but its influence can none the less prove distracting and detrimental. It may be that the counsellor has had a phone conversation with the potential client and that this has sown the seeds of dislike or attraction or even the beginnings of a 'diagnosis'. The address of the client or, if the counsellor is institution-based, the client's work role or position in the hierarchy may evoke fantasies or stimulate attitudes in the counsellor. Most difficult of all can be the situation where the client has been referred by another person or agency so that the counsellor is in possession of a detailed referral letter or even a whole dossier of material about the client and his past life. In the face of such a welter of information the counsellor may experience grave problems in receiving the client with an open mind, and indeed of seeing him at all except through the distorting spectacles of other people's judgements and, not infrequently, of their impotence and frustration. Small wonder, then, that most experienced person-centred practitioners cultivate the art of deafness and blindness to other people's judgements about potential clients and even seek to hold at arm's length their own premature impressions which are usually based on fragmented and unreliable data. Referral letters need to be treated with caution and may be best kept for after the first session, and if it turns out that the client is expecting the counsellor to know all about him the counsellor needs to be honest that she does not possess such knowledge and that she has deliberately refrained from knowing because she wishes their meeting to be uncontaminated by other people's interpretations. This is a new relationship and she wishes to experience it in all its freshness.

Box 6.1 What Messages does my Counselling Service Give?

How warm and welcoming is the written material about my service?
Does it over-emphasise my authority?

How is my answerphone message received by others?

What does my waiting room say?
Does it say that I am out of date like my magazines?
Does it say that my service is shoddy like its furnishings?
Does it say that we like the set-up well enough to put fresh flowers in the waiting room?
Is my information board up to date and interesting enough to occupy the client who wants to be occupied?

How does my receptionist respond to clients?
Is he/she warm?
Does he/she really help them to feel that it is OK to be there?
Is he/she sensitive to clients who need to be left alone and to those who need a bit of attention?
Can he/she respond to the client in crisis?
Does he/she know the kinds of situations when it is important that he/she interrupt me?
Does he/she need more of my caring and attention?

What does my counselling room say to clients?
Does it convey warmth, or is it cold and clinical?
Why is that certificate of mine on the wall? How far is it there for my clients or for me? Does it give confidence? Or does it remind clients that I am the expert?
What else does my room divulge about me (through posters, paintings, books, etc.)? Is that OK?
Is there a chair which is obviously 'mine' in the sense that it is more comfortable or higher than the others?
Are there any tables or other obstacles between me and the client?
Is the positioning of the furniture such that my client feels that I am not unduly close and yet I am close enough to hear every whisper and also to touch without undue disruption?

The expectations which clients have of counselling and counsellors are many and varied and not a few will be at variance with the counsellor's own understanding of her task. Some clients may come expecting to be told what to do or be offered authoritative advice. Others, again, may expect a barrage of questions leading to a diagnosis of the problem. Yet others may be old hands at the therapeutic game and may come expecting little help but hoping against all the odds that this particular helper will be different. The counsellor can make no assumptions about her client's expectations but she can be sure that, unless these are to some extent revealed and explored in the early days of a therapeutic relationship, there will be grave difficulties later on. Everything again points to the essential desirability of the counsellor being able to be open, attentive, receptive, without assumptions, as she greets her new client for the first time and the door of the counselling room closes behind them.

THE FIRST MOMENTS

The counsellor knows the room, the client does not. The counsellor is well versed in the counselling activity, the client may be complete novice. The counsellor is buttressed by her experience and knowledge, the client is likely to be vulnerable and in some distress. In short, at this opening moment this is a strikingly unequal encounter. The counsellor holds nearly all the cards in a game of which the client does not even know the rules. For the person-centred counsellor this clear imbalance of power will be a matter of immediate and pressing concern. Somehow the client must be enabled to feel that he has not relinquished all control over his situation and put himself in an inferior position where he has no option but to be submissive and dependent. The counsellor will be at pains to do all she can to redress the power balance. Different counsellors develop their own individual ways of giving signals of warmth and equality. For instance one of the writers was influenced by his experience of a Japanese tea ceremony, and since then he has made a point of offering coffee to every client at the start of a session unless it is obvious that the client's crisis is too pressing. Pouring coffee for a client has become an initial, unconditional gift and mark of respect.

Pacing is important at the outset. An unhurried pace indicates that there is space to breathe, a certain freedom in the air. The counsellor's opening statement will be likely to reinforce further that it is the client's hour and that he has the freedom to use it for his own needs. The counsellor does not have a preconceived plan or structure into which the client must fit. The only structure may be the length of time which can be spent together on this occasion and the counsellor may well make that explicit. Once, then, the client has chosen a chair and is sitting down with an air of expectancy the counsellor will begin:

Well, we have about fifty minutes together now. How can I be of help?

Sometimes, of course, no introductory words at all are necessary, for the client immediately bursts into tears or begins with a torrent of words which he has been holding back perhaps for days. Should this happen the counsellor will be content to give the client full attention and to follow where he leads. She will not attempt to intervene or to impose her own structure on the interaction. Some years ago one of the writers received a young female student who began to weep in the opening seconds of the first interview and who continued to cry for the following forty minutes. The counsellor merely waited attentively and after a few minutes gently took the client's hand and held it. At the end of the forty minutes the girl looked up, smiled through her tears and said: 'Thank you. I feel better now.' And she left without the counsellor having said a single word.

Sometimes the client's opening statements will reveal his expectations of the counselling process – or his lack of them. To the open-ended question 'How can I help you?' he may well reply. 'I'm not sure: perhaps you can't' or 'I would like you to give me your advice', or 'I just need someone who'll help me put things in perspective', or 'I've never been to a counsellor before. What do you do?', or 'I'm at the end of my tether. Someone's got to help me.' Whatever the reply the counsellor will be alerted to the client's expectations and needs and will be intent on understanding them so that she can relate to them and, if necessary, disabuse the client of expectations which are inappropriate or impossible to fulfil.

For the person-centred counsellor the task is always the same even if the response can take a hundred different forms. It is to 'level' with the client, to show him that he is worthy of absolute attention, that he merits every effort the counsellor can make to understand him, that he is perceived as a fellow human being who, for that reason alone, can be assured of the counsellor's acceptance and honesty. In the light of this overriding task it is instructive to track the varying responses which the counsellor might offer to the opening client statements quoted above. 'I'm not sure: perhaps you can't' might elicit: 'You're not really sure that I shall be of much use'. Or 'There's a real doubt in your mind about having come.'

Both these responses show that the counsellor's main concern is to indicate to her client that she really has heard what he has said and is not concerned to establish her own agenda or to offer what could only be facile assurance at such an early stage.

'I would like you to give me your advice' poses a more difficult problem for the counsellor. She knows that she is not in the business of advice-giving and that to be placed in such a role could be counterproductive. At the same time she may not wish to risk a response which could be seen by the client as an immediate put-down. She may opt for: 'You feel you need some guidance' or 'Perhaps, together, we can see what might be a way forward.' Or, most likely, she may regard the remark as simply an ice-breaker and merely nod or smile. Should it become apparent that the client really does expect her to offer authoritative instruction, or to tell him what to do, she will need gently to unravel this expectation as the session proceeds.

The client who opens with: 'I just need someone who'll help me get this in perspective' presents the counsellor with the dilemma of whether to respond to the role issue or to the veiled content implicit in the statement – or, indeed, to both: 'I shall be happy to help you see things more clearly', indicates the willingness of the counsellor to be the kind of mirror which the client seems to be requesting. 'You feel things have got somewhat out of proportion' acknowledges the client's fear that he has lost objective balance while: 'Perhaps together we can try to find the perspective you feel you've lost,' attempts to cope with both aspects of the client's statement.

Already in some of the possible counsellor responses the central issue of equality has been hinted at. As rapidly as possible the counsellor will wish in the interests of honesty and clarity to dispel the illusion that she will assume the role of expert in the client's life. The concept of co-operation and of 'coming alongside' in order that the necessary 'work' can be undertaken together needs to be established, although the counsellor, as always, will strive to be sensitive to the given moment and will not allow a preoccupation with these role issues to ride roughshod over a client's more pressing needs. It would be paramountly absurd, for example, to deliver a homily about working together if a client is shaking from head to foot and can scarcely string two words together.

The rare client who actually asks at the very beginning for a definition of roles and tasks is, in some ways, a counsellor's dream. Theoretically, of course, all clients should have addressed this issue before coming if they have read the agency's brochure or the counsellor's published statement about her work. In reality few do and those who have are unlikely to have internalised the implications for their own relationship with the counsellor. It is therefore worth reflecting on the likely response to the occasional client who says: 'I've never been to a counsellor before. What do you do?' As is almost invariably the case the counsellor has a number of options. She might decide to respond to the feelings behind the question: 'It's important to you to know how I work' or, as is likely at this opening moment, she might well take the question at its face value and try to answer it. Again, she might wish to check out with the client whether he wishes to explore this issue thoroughly: 'Would you like us to talk about that at some length before we get started?' If she chooses the second option she is likely to say something like: 'I see my task as helping you to express what's on your mind so that you can perhaps begin to see things more clearly. And I really am concerned to try to understand what's going on for you.' Such a response is tackling a number of important issues in a highly concise way. In the first place the emphasis is placed firmly on the client's responsibility to move towards greater clarity with the counsellor's help. Secondly, there is an acknowledgement that to 'express what's on your mind' is not necessarily an easy thing to do and may require skilled help.' Thirdly, the counsellor's final remark stresses the paramount significance which she attaches to understanding and indicates ('really am concerned') her preparedness to commit herself to this task. Should the client have made it clear that he really does want a kind of mini-seminar before begin-ning the counselling work the likelihood is that the counsellor will talk at much greater length about the nature of the relationship which she hopes they may be able to achieve, and of her central belief in the capacity of individuals to find their own inner resources to cope with life's challenges. She may also explicitly state her willingness to stay alongside her client for as long as seems necessary and appropriate to both of them. Certainly there will be no reluctance on the counsellor's part to spell out to the client all those aspects of the counselling relationship and activities which seem to require elucidation. She will be at pains to make it clear that she has no desire to retreat behind a professional smokescreen or to impress the client with psychotherapeutic jargon or mystique. On the contrary, her message will be that she wishes to be as honest and transparent as she can be about the counselling process, and that she is prepared to go to considerable lengths to convey this if that is what the client appears to want at the outset.

ESTABLISHING TRUST

The length of the *beginning* phase of counselling is directly related to the *readiness* of the client at the outset. Some clients arrive in counselling at a time when they are ready to take responsibility for their life and willing to trust an unknown process. Other clients may be making a beginning before this sense of responsibility and trust is well-formed (see Box 6.2).

There is no magic formula and perhaps only two general rules – namely, that the process can never be hurried and that the counsellor's commitment is always to the consistent offering of the core conditions and to the equalising of power within the relationship. The client's 'readiness' will affect the speed with which trust develops in the relationship, and the establishment of this trust is what will ultimately determine the level and quality of work which can be undertaken. In our case-study, which begins at the end of this chapter, the client's 'readiness' was so great that, despite relatively poor work by the counsellor, both people were swept into a depth of intimacy in only the second meeting. In other cases it may be weeks or months before sufficient trust is established to permit the first stumbling steps forward together.

There are some who would maintain that even the opening statement suggested earlier: 'Well, we have about fifty minutes together now. How can I be of help?' already colludes with a power imbalance. The very idea that the counsellor is there to help and that the client is the one to be helped has about it the whiff of a superiority/inferiority equation. There may well be something in this objection as far as certain clients are concerned, and Box 6.3 presents a range of other possibilities all of which strive to avoid completely the trap of implying role definitions while at the same time offering a welcoming and unclinical invitation to an as yet unknown fellow human being.

All the responses presented in Box 6.3 share one element in common. They avoid small talk. No attempt is made to put a client at ease by discussing the weather, by alluding to the journey he may have made in order to be present or by discussing the state of the nation. Perhaps there may very occasionally be a case for resorting to such strategies, but in most instances a moment's reflection will reveal that a client's major concern is to embark at once on an exploration of his reason for coming. In such circumstances discussing the weather or other irrelevances usually heightens rather than alleviates anxiety and tension and sets an inappropriate norm of superficiality right at the beginning.

Box 6.2 The Client's State of Readiness for Counselling

Here are five elements which can denote a *low* 'state of readiness' in a client. None of these would make counselling impossible, but their presence or absence may lengthen or shorten the beginning of the counselling process.

Indecision about wanting to change:
'I'd like my relationship with my wife to be different but not if it creates too much upset.'

General lack of trust for others:
'People say they want to help me but really they want to help themselves.'

Unwillingness to take responsibility for self in life:
'It's nothing to do with me – it's this depression that makes me do these things.'

Unwillingness to take responsibility in counselling:
'It's your job to cure me – now get on with it!'

Unwillingness to recognise or explore feelings:
'Yes, I feel sad about it, but focusing on bad feelings never did anyone any good.'

Box 6.3 A Range of Counsellor Opening Statements

1   We have about fifty minutes now. How would you like to use the time together?
2   Well, what has brought you here? We have about fifty minutes now for us to use.
3   We have fifty minutes or so together now. Let me know what brings you here.
4   Well, where would you like to start? We have about fifty minutes now.
5   When you're ready please feel free to start where you want.
6   You have my full attention. It's over to you to let me know how you want to use the time we have.
7   [*Smiles*] Hello, then. It's all yours. Where would you like to begin?
8   [*Smiles*] How can I be of use to you?

The importance of starting immediately is clear in the case of a client in crisis. The client response – 'I'm at the end of my tether. Someone's got to help me' – is just such an example of a client in crisis. In the face of such an opening statement the counsellor clearly needs immediately to move into a deeply empathic mode.

The client in crisis needs above all else to know that his feelings are received and understood, and that he is being taken with the utmost seriousness. This does not mean, of course, that the counsellor will be swept into the crisis herself. Indeed, the very activity of empathic understanding often has the effect of defusing a crisis, of slowing down the pace and relieving to some extent the crippling sense of anxiety and dread which the client may be undergoing.

The experience of being deeply understood and the sense of companionship which springs from this are in themselves powerful antidotes to the overwhelming feelings of panic and powerlessness which can be the concomitants of crisis. If the client in crisis is to endow the counselling process with trust he is more likely to do so if the counsellor's empathic ability is well to the fore from the opening seconds. Box 6.4 illustrates such an opening.

Box 6.4 The Crisis Client and the Empathic Beginning

COUNSELLOR: How can I be of use to you?

CLIENT: My sixteen-year-old son has been killed in a road smash – yesterday – I just can't face it. I feel I'm going mad. I'm caught in a nightmare.

COUNSELLOR: [puts her hand on the client's knee] You just don't know how you are going to cope with what must be the most appalling thing that's ever happened to you. You feel you're going out of your mind.

CLIENT: [collapses sobbing into the counsellor's arms]

It is likely that an opening session which begins with such a dramatic and empathic interchange will quickly develop an intensity of relationship which leads to a high level of client self-disclosure. Indeed, the more the counsellor empathises accurately, the more likelihood there is of this occurring. There is a danger when a relationship accelerates at such breakneck speed that the client will subsequently feel that he has exposed himself too shamelessly and with indecent haste. The skilled counsellor will be alert to this possibility and may well attempt to forewarn the client of such feelings: 'We have shared a lot today and you have been very open with me. I want you to know that I feel fine about that just in case you feel later that you've said too much. I am sure it was right to jump in at the deep end.' The establishing of trust in a relationship is a delicate and complex process and inappropriate feelings of shame can be a major stumbling block to its consolidation.

In sharp contrast to the crisis client, the 'hardened' client who may well have visited a whole gamut of psychiatric and helping services challenges the counsellor in quite different ways. Such a person is likely to be swift to discern inauthenticity and to be well accustomed to the application of mechanistic counselling techniques. In short, he will be concerned to gauge the counsellor's genuineness and willingness to engage in a non-defensive way. Not surprisingly such clients can sometimes seem cynical and aggressive. Box 6.5 indicates the kind of opening exchanges which are not untypical and which test the counsellor's congruence from the outset.

Box 6.5 The 'Hardened' Client and the Congruent Beginning

COUNSELLOR: We have about fifty minutes now. How would you like to begin?

CLIENT: The therapeutic hour, eh?

COUNSELLOR: That's right.

CLIENT: God knows where to begin. You people are all the same. You expect me to do all the bloody work.

COUNSELLOR: I feel that's a bit rough. You've only known me for thirty seconds. But you reckon all counsellors are idle sods, do you, who force you to do all the difficult bits?

CLIENT: Something like that, I suppose. But admit it, you aren't going to give me any answers, are you?

COUNSELLOR: I doubt it, but I'm beginning to relish the prospect of wrestling around with you to find some answers. I'm game to have a go if you're willing to take the risk.

To such clients even genuine empathy may be seen as contrived and stilted, and the counsellor will do well to stay firmly in touch with her own feelings and to be ready to express them even if they seem combative or unaccepting. Hardened clients have often experienced helpers who had no real interest in them, or helpers who constantly ducked behind the helping role and disappeared into frightened anonymity. Above all they are seeking a counsellor who is prepared to be open with them and whose identity is strong enough not to be shaken by their apparent aggressiveness or overt cynicism.

Some clients are so deeply self-rejecting when they first cross the counsellor's threshold that they are close to self-destruction. They feel worthless, rejected, without hope. In such cases it is the counsellor's attitude of unconditional positive regard which comes to the fore. This is not to say that empathy and congruence are irrelevant; simply that, for the deeply self-rejecting client the most active ingredient for the fostering of trust is likely to be the counsellor's warm and unconditional regard. What is more it may well be that such an attitude will have to be maintained over many weeks before the client can begin dimly to sense that it is strong and enduring. Such clients are often fearful that it is only a question of time before the counsellor's patience and warmth will run out, and they will be asked, politely, to seek help elsewhere. When it eventually dawns on them that this is not going to happen then the scene is set for them to make the first tentative move to climb out of the pit of self-negation. They begin to catch at least a germ or two of the counsellor's acceptance of them. One of the writers has on his wall – out of sight of all but the most inquisitive clients – a remarkable poem by Richard Church which begins 'Learning to wait consumes my life / Consumes and feeds as well', and this discipline of 'learning to wait' is a prerequisite in the face of the self-rejecting client. Without such a discipline, based on the deep belief in each individual's inner resources, there is little likelihood that the person-centred counsellor will be able to maintain, without portrayal, the consistent warmth and unconditionality of regard which alone can bring some of the most deeply distressed clients to the point of trusting the therapeutic relationship.

'DISGUISES' AND 'CLUES'

The inner world of a human being is a sanctuary, and it is therefore scarcely surprising that many clients grant admission only after much deliberation. When the client hesitantly takes the initiative to move to a deeper level he may well do so in a somewhat ambiguous fashion. Especially in the early stages of a relationship, he may appear, in fact, to be giving double messages. Such behaviour is readily understandable, for the client can have no guarantee that the counsellor will be able to respond effectively to material which has not yet been revealed. He does not know whether the more intense feelings, the raw needs and fears or the confusion or violence will drive the counsellor away. It is likely that such aspects of himself have driven other people away in the past. One strategy which the client may therefore choose to employ is to adopt a kind of '*disguise*'. This behaviour indicates the need for the client to 'hedge his bets' so that in the event of the counsellor proving to be inadequate to respond at a deeper level he can readily retreat into the disguise without having suffered the consequences of rendering himself too vulnerable. Such a process is usually not wholly conscious on the part of the client and most commonly falls just beyond the edge of his awareness.

In the early stages of a counselling relationship one of the most common 'disguises' is the cloak of humour when the client lets slip an important message but dresses the words up in apparent flippancy or accompanies them with laughter. In such an instance the counsellor is left with the choice of responding to the important message or to the humorous packaging. An example of such a situation is the client who says, laughing as he does so, 'and I even get depressed about it sometimes – imagine that, me, depressed!' This kind of double message is telling evidence of how sophisticated the human being can be in his self-defence. If the counsellor proves unable to respond at the deeper level, or responds in an unacceptable fashion, the client can readily fall back on the disguise and imply that it was the central message: 'Don't take me seriously; I was enjoying the joke, you know.'

Another common strategy which falls into the same category is for a client to convey a message of substance but to do so with a choice of words which makes it sound much less important. An example of this 'diluting' choice of words would occur if a highly depressed person spoke of himself as 'feeling a bit low sometimes' or a desperately lonely individual commented 'but it's not so bad really because everyone gets lonely at times'. It is likely that we have all developed our own particular repertoire of preferred disguises and although a few, like those mentioned above, are very common, part of the counsellor's task at the beginning of a relationship is to discover the particular repertoire of the new client. This is an aspect of what we have described elsewhere as appreciating the client's 'personal language' (see Chapter 4).

Sometimes it is not the client's actual words which indicate his desire to move to a deeper level but some non-verbal '*clue*' which suggests that this important change could be made. The clue might be an unnaturally long pause, a change in the tone of voice, or a shift in eye contact. In just the same way as with disguises, the counsellor has the opportunity to accept the clue or not, and the client can acknowledge the existence of the clue or not. Sometimes the inexperienced helper may notice the clue but will decide that she does not wish to go to a deeper level, perhaps for fear of entering terrain where she doubts her own ability to cope. Or, again, it may be the client who decides that the counsellor's response is inadequate. In either case both may stay at the more superficial level. The social skill involved in such an exchange is truly marvellous: an invitation has been offered and either rejected or not accepted whole-heartedly enough, and all this has been conducted at a level of communication which neither need acknowledge. No matter what happens both parties can maintain 'face', and this can be of particular importance for the client in the beginning stages of a counselling relationship.

THE END OF THE BEGINNING

Much of this chapter has been concerned with first sessions or even opening moments in a counsellor-client relationship, but it will by now be clear that the beginning phase usually extends well beyond the first session and cannot be expressed in terms of any particular time duration. We have made much of the establishing of trust in the relationship, and perhaps this must ultimately be the criterion which determines the point when the end of the beginning has been reached. At the stage when the client feels that he can trust the relationship sufficiently to take the risk of moving into unknown or half-known territory it can be said that the therapeutic journey is under way and the counsellor's companionship has been welcomed and endorsed. For some clients such a point, as we have seen, may be reached after thirty seconds, while for others it may be months before this critical phase is completed. It is this wide variation in the time required for trust to develop that has a crucial bearing on the structures which need to be agreed at the outset of the counselling relationship.

STRUCTURES AND CONTRACTS

As the end of a first session approaches counsellor and client are faced with the problem of what to do next. It is, of course, possible that the only thing that needs to be done is to bring the relationship to a positive and satisfactory conclusion. After all there *are* some concerns and problems

121

which can be appropriately explored and even resolved in the space of a fifty-minute interview! (Talmon, 1990). Another reason for ending with the first session is where the client is not satisfied with the appropriateness of what the counsellor is offering. Perhaps the client has expected a more instantaneous 'solution', or seeks a relationship where the counsellor is a more powerful figure. Issues such as these can be important content during the initial session but they can also indicate a rapid ending even though the counsellor may regard it as premature (see Chapter 8). If the work is going to continue it is desirable that, at an early stage in the relationship, probably at the end of the first session, the implications of this are fully addressed. It is important for both client and counsellor that they have some sense of the nature of the commitment to each other on which they are about to embark.

There are likely to be a number of different options possible and, as always in the person-centred tradition, the counsellor will be concerned to ensure that she does not impose a structure on the client but that they work out a mutually acceptable arrangement for their work together. It is not uncommon for counsellor and client to agree on a provisional contract of a certain number of sessions. They might, for example, decide to meet weekly on four more occasions and then take stock. There is nothing intrinsically inappropriate about this kind of arrangement as long as it is clear from the outset that at the end of the agreed number of sessions it is the client and not the counsellor who will have the deciding say on whether or not to continue for a longer period. Many clients who present themselves for counselling have experienced such rejection and invalidation at the hands of others that it is only too likely that they will interpret the offer of a four-session contract as the counsellor's polite way of ensuring that she does not have to put up with them for more than a month. The policy of leaving the ultimate decision to the client about whether or not to continue does not, of course, mean that the counsellor forfeits her right to voice her own thoughts and feelings when the time comes to take stock. If she believes that the relationship is unproductive, or that little more is likely to be achieved she will say so, and her feelings will then become an important ingredient in the decision-making process. She will not, however, start from the basic assumption that she is right and that she knows better than her client. In our experience it has never happened that such provisional contracts end in a situation where the client wishes strongly to continue and the counsellor wishes strongly to terminate. If such an apparent impasse should ever arise it is our belief that the counsellor should attempt to continue at least for a while with all the support she can muster from her supervisor.

Instead of employing a provisional contract the counsellor and client may opt for a more open-ended arrangement whereby they agree to go on meeting for as long as seems necessary. It is likely that a somewhat imprecise time scale will be mentioned – a few weeks, a month or two, or, where the difficulties seem particularly severe, a few months perhaps. Such an arrangement is often much better suited to those clients who are highly anxious or fearful of rejection, or conscious that they have been sitting on a whole mass of distress for years. Again, however, it is essential that they know from the outset that the counsellor is not retaining the power to terminate the relationship when she feels it should end, but that they have the primary role in determining their own therapeutic need. Such open-ended arrangements can often benefit from periodic review sessions which will be much the same in nature as those occurring at the end of provisional contracts. These, too, can be agreed in principle at the outset and will become a natural part of the therapeutic process with either client or counsellor feeling free to introduce them.

The frequency of sessions needs also to be decided at an early stage, and here again the person-centred counsellor will be keen to avoid too much rigidity. It is likely that the weekly session of fifty minutes will be appropriate enough for most clients but there is nothing sacrosanct about this particular structure. The client who initially arrives in a state of dire crisis may well require more frequent meetings at first (possibly of a shorter duration), whereas there are others who may welcome a longer period between sessions. Certainly there is every likelihood that as counselling proceeds the frequency agreed at the beginning will seem no longer appropriate. The duration of sessions, too, may change. Both writers have experienced some counselling relationships where clients have wanted and benefited from sessions lasting two or three hours or even longer. It is also not uncommon for a few clients to find themselves becoming more comfortable with longer sessions at less frequent intervals. At the beginning stage, however, what needs to be established is the willingness of the counsellor to be open about both the duration and the frequency of sessions no matter what structure is initially adopted. In practice, it is the exception rather than the rule for a client to desire a radical change of structure but the knowledge at the outset that such changes are at least *possible is* often of some importance to many clients. It is yet another sign that the counsellor is willing to share power and to be responsive to her client's needs even if these change in ways which are potentially inconvenient to her.

It will be evident from much that has preceded that person-centred counsellors will find it difficult to work in agencies where policy dictates that clients can have a certain number of sessions and no more. Such a system takes away power from both counsellor and client, and it is only by acknowledging, accepting and transcending such shared impotence that a person-centred counsellor and her client could work constructively together. We do not believe this to be impossible but such policies certainly present formidable obstacles to person-centred work. Where they operate in order to cope with unmanageable numbers of clients it is clear that lack of resources is the real problem. When they are introduced on the grounds that short intensive therapeutic relationships produce good results we are unhappy. Clearly such short-term counselling can and often does prove highly beneficial, but we find it unlikely that such can be the case for all clients.

There is an important difference between 'short-term' and 'time-limited' counselling. Agency counsellors, particularly those working in primary care, have felt under pressure to conform to a 'time-limited' convention whereby they may offer no more than a fixed number of sessions, with no flexibility. This kind of policy pays no regard to individual difference among clients and is a crude and inefficient way of structuring a counselling provision. For a start, stipulating the limit of, say eight sessions, at the beginning of counselling can set that as a *target* in the mind of the client, where three or four sessions might otherwise have sufficed. Also, it can be uneconomic to end prematurely with a client when he is at a point of particular readiness. Disregarding points of readiness, where the client's condition is acute, is expensive when it results in later chronicity. The alternative, which is equally respectful of budgets, is to consider the work as 'short-term' but not time-limited. For example, in primary health care, nothing is time-limited, but everything is short-term. Under this system the counselling service might contract to offer an *average* of, say, six sessions per client. This system still allows the quantity of service to be contained and predicted, but it allows counsellors much more scope to sculpt their practice to invest 'savings' from those clients who required only two or three sessions in other clients with whom stopping at six sessions would represent an expensive waste of time. This latter model is also better for counsellors, who can then generate a range of experience comprising mainly short-term contracts but also some medium and even longer-term work (Mearns, 1998b). Many of the issues raised by what is, in fact, a crucial matter with many financial and clinical implications are addressed in a recent keynote lecture given by one of the writers (Thorne) at the annual training conference of the British Association for Counselling (Thorne, 1999).

Money Matters

For counsellors working in private practice or in fee-paying agencies the question of money has to be faced at an early stage with each new client. In some cases the agency absolves the counsellor from any responsibility in this area by determining the fee and by billing the account. Very often, however, the counsellor herself must incorporate the payment issue into the first session and this is not always easy, especially if the client is highly distressed or there has been some difficulty in sorting out times and frequency of subsequent meetings. The issue cannot, however, be dodged and it demands straightforward openness and directness. It is important that the client is not left with uncertainties and ambiguities. He needs to know exactly how much he has to pay (if there is some kind of sliding scale he needs to know the ramifications of this) and he needs to know what happens if he fails to turn up for an appointment without giving warning. The counsellor for her part will be concerned to understand the client's feelings about financial aspects of the relationship – especially if there are difficult feelings around – and she will be likely to offer whatever options are possible for the mode of payment. It is our experience that very often it is the counsellor who experiences great discomfort about the financial transaction rather than the client, and that such unease often springs from a lurking self-doubt about her competence or even a somewhat shaky faith in the effectiveness of the counselling process itself. It is often these issues which the counsellor needs to address in supervision rather than other 'ethical' misgivings about charging for services which may be serving as a smokescreen for the more fundamental doubts about personal and professional identity. A final point to note about payment is the importance of the counsellor working for a fee which is neither so low that she feels 'used' or so high that she feels that she has to 'perform' well to live up to that figure.

Summary

We make no apology for subjecting the beginnings of counselling relationships to such rigorous examination, or for dwelling on such apparently trivial matters as furniture and out-of-date magazines. It is well known that first impressions have profound significance for all of us in many different aspects of our lives, and it is therefore scarcely surprising that there are those who claim that the likely outcome of a therapeutic relationship can often be predicted from the quality of interaction which takes place during the first two or three sessions. For the person-centred counsellor everything she says and does, everything about the environment which she offers her client, everything about the structures that are agreed at the outset of the work together – all this will be attempting to convey the same unambiguous message: 'I welcome you, I accept and value you as a human being, I want to understand you, I want us to be able to be open and honest with each other and there is nothing in me that wants to take anything away from you. And my hope is that we shall be able to work together for as long as you feel it to be helpful and worthwhile.'

THE CASE-STUDY (PART 1)

Introduction

We are arbitrarily defining the 'beginning' phase of the counselling process as the period during which the client develops sufficient trust in the counsellor and their relationship to explore the previously feared edges of his awareness. There is no single path which the therapeutic process must take in order to develop this trust; rather, there are many 'roads to success' as counsellor and client move forward towards the next phase of their therapeutic encounter.

In the first part of the case-study which follows we trace one such 'road' through the beginning of the counselling process. This is a single case and as such it cannot reflect all the points we have made in this chapter. Nonetheless we hope it will highlight much of what it means for a counsellor and client to find sufficient courage and trust in each other to set out together on their unpredictable journey.

In describing a case a major problem is deciding what to leave out. In the account which follows we have tried to retain only material which both client or counsellor felt had been of particular significance. As a result, many meetings and events receive only brief comment to allow more space for exploring moments which radically affected the process.

Data from a number of sources have been used in the case presentation, which is the outcome of work undertaken by both counsellor and client some two years after counselling had ended. Firstly, audio-tape recordings were available for all seventeen sessions. The second major source of information was the client, Joan. She had kept a sketchy diary during the period of counselling and was able to use this, together with the audio-tapes, to write detailed notes on how she had experienced the four-month counselling process. She was asked to comment on each of the seventeen sessions and also to take into account any insights which had occurred between meetings.

The third source of data was the counsellor's notes about the case. In person-centred case-studies, attention is given not just to the material the *client* brings and her behaviour in counselling, but also to the counsellor's experience of *himself* during the contact, as well as the counsellor's judgement on the quality and intensity of the therapeutic *relationship*. Hence case-notes of person-centred practitioners normally contain these three dimensions of 'client', 'self', and 'the relationship'. Such detailed case-notes were available for the first ten meetings but were more sparse thereafter. Some of the notes have been re-written in sentence form and are reproduced in the case presentation.

After Joan and the counsellor had reconstructed their individual experiences of the counselling process they came together to compare their perceptions and in this way created a further source of data. During this comparing experience Joan and the counsellor frequently referred back to the tape-recordings for clarification. These meetings threw up many examples of differences in understanding, including the discovery of assumptions which the counsellor had made about the client's experience which turned out to be spurious. This close collaboration between counsellor and client ensures that the description of the counselling process which follows represents their agreed account, and not simply the counsellor's gloss on events.

The Context

The setting for this case is a private counselling practice. At the time the counselling took place Joan was twenty-seven years old. She was married to Roger, had no children, and was engaged in voluntary social work. Her mother was dead and she had lost contact with her father. Joan had been referred by a former client and made her appointment directly with the counsellor by telephone. During that telephone conversation Joan introduced the matter of fees. The counsellor had pointed to his normal policy, which was to have two fees: the higher for clients who could afford it and the other set somewhat lower for those in financial difficulty. The counsellor also mentioned that his policy was not to charge for the first session if the client chose not to continue. Joan decided to pay the higher fee and said that she wanted to pay for the first session regardless of whether they continued or not. During this telephone conversation the counsellor informed Joan that sessions were not rigidly timed, but were never less than one hour, and usually ended before one and a quarter hours.

Another relevant part of the context is the state of being of the counsellor during the first session. This is of particular importance in the case under discussion because the counsellor was feeling drained and somewhat unsettled at the time. The addition of Joan brought his case-load up to its maximum and he wondered after the telephone call whether he should have been more cautious before accepting her. Another issue that was unsettling for the counsellor was his difficulty at that time with a particularly demanding client called Christine. Clients sometimes go through a period of being challenging and demanding, but the counsellor was having more difficulty than usual with Christine and her repeated demands to 'prove you can do a good job', combined with a seemingly constant stream of criticism. This difficulty was to exercise an undesirable influence on the opening sessions with Joan.

Meeting 1

This first meeting lasted one and a quarter hours, and it is interesting to note that in their reflections two years later the counsellor and client focused on exactly the same events as being particularly significant. We begin with Joan's account of the experience.

When I came to his office I was very scared. I was putting a brave face on it, but this was really a matter of life or death for me . . . And he was a stranger . . . in a sense I was about to trust my life to a stranger.

Just as I got inside the door and he moved towards me, he met my gaze with a flicker in his eyes as if he was nervous. I thought – 'Oh, God, he's not going to be strong enough for me!' In the first five minutes I wanted to run out of the door, but I just couldn't – so I kept on talking. I don't think I *showed* much feeling. That changed when he said, 'You look very tense – are you scared? . . . is *this* scary?' I can hear on the tape that I let out a huge sigh of relief, and I remember I looked at him for the first time since I had sat down.

Much of the remainder of this meeting was devoted to Joan telling her story. She spoke about how she felt 'a prisoner' in her life – how she 'can't escape' – how she felt that she was 'dying in this marriage'. She referred to her husband Roger as 'feelingless' and she was intensely bitter at the fact that he seemed unable to respond to her emotion. She described in some detail the sado-masochistic practices which had begun early in their relationship. She felt that she rushed into marriage because she was 'scared to do anything else'. Two years previously she had had an affair, but had 'obeyed' Roger when he demanded that she end it. She said that she had felt 'paralysed by guilt' and the only possible course of action was to return to the marriage to 'try again'. In talking about this return to the marriage, she said: 'At one level I knew it wouldn't work, but I denied that to myself'.

Joan describes how it felt to tell her story in counselling:

> By the end of the first session I had told most of my story. At times I
> went so fast that he [the counsellor] didn't have a chance to come in. I
> think that was the only way I could tell my story – I couldn't face the
> *feeling* that was involved in it. Also I went fast and didn't look at him
> much, in case he put me off . . . in case I saw that he was disapproving
> or rejecting me.

Near the end of this meeting the counsellor quite firmly stopped Joan's flow of speech and took time carefully and deliberately to show his interest, warmth and understanding with a strongly *affirming* statement:

> You have told me an awful lot about yourself today. I have seen how
> scary it is to do that and also I've seen how important it is for you to
> do that. I have been in *awe* of your courage – you're sure not letting go
> without a fight.

In this account of the first meeting we have paid particular attention to the *client* and the material which she brought. However, as mentioned earlier, the person-centred counsellor is also concerned with monitoring *himself* and the development of his *relationship* with the client. Hence, we reproduce below the counsellor's reflections on these after this first meeting.

> SELF: As I focus on myself in this first session with Joan I am aware
> that I was quite nervous in the beginning. At first sight she seemed
> very intense and severe, with eyes that looked right through me. I
> was taken aback with her intensity and took some time to settle.
> Her long monologue at the beginning gave me the space to

become more centred and to focus on *her.* It sort of feels like I actually felt *fear* towards her in the first moment and only when I focused on her did that slide and change to a real prizing of her in her struggle.

RELATIONSHIP: I think the most important moment was near the end when I stopped her flow to strongly and clearly show her how much I admired her courage. That affirmation might be important for her in relation to her struggle but I suspect it will also help to strengthen her trust and our relationship. I feel very positive about the potential for our relationship but I suspect that she is quite wary of making a commitment. It will be important for me to make a particular effort to *communicate* my respect and my understanding. I think she might not believe me unless I say it really strongly.

Meeting 2

This meeting began with the counsellor asking the question: 'What is most prominent for you just now?' Joan went on to talk about how much better she felt after the last meeting – all week she had felt stronger. She says: 'I hope it doesn't go away . . . I hope it works . . .'

We continue the account from the counsellor's notes:

At this point I made a mistake which was later recovered and ended in significant movement for our therapeutic relationship. As Joan said 'I hope it works' I was struck by her gaze, which seemed so penetrating. I became edgy and uncomfortable and I moved back in my seat as though I was under some threat. In a flash I thought about the hard time Christine had been giving me and how I was not coping at all well with that. I began to wonder if Joan was also desperately scared that I might fail her. Within a few moments I had become completely uncentred and found it difficult to put this theory to the back of my mind so that I could devote my full attention to listening to what Joan was saying. After a short silence I decided to face my uncertainty by commenting on what I saw in Joan's appearance in that moment. I did not reflect my deeper experiencing of her since I knew that was likely to be contaminated by the intrusion of my experience of Christine, so I said . . . [*continued from tapes*].

COUNSELLOR: I hope it works? . . . When you say that, you look so tense . . . and so *in*tense . . . is there more to say on that . . . do you have any more feelings that go with that?

[*Long pause*].

JOAN: Yes . . . fear . . . no . . . *terror*! I'm terrified. I'm absolutely terrified.

[*Pause*].

COUNSELLOR [*in a soft, slow and warm voice*]: What are you terrified about, Joan?

JOAN: I'm terrified that you will desert me.

[*Continued from the counsellor's notes*]

This amazed me – I didn't see it coming at all. I was so contaminated by my experience with Christine that I had feared Joan might similarly be terrified lest I not be *powerful* enough for her. In fact Joan's terror was quite differently based – she was terrified I would *desert* her. I am glad that I was suspicious about my initial reaction and took care to check it out.

Joan continues the story of this second meeting by recalling that moment when she divulged her terror of desertion.

This moment in our second meeting was critical for me. I remember that I was absolutely flooded with feelings after I said I was terrified of rejection. As well as feeling that this was my last chance for life and that I might be rejected, I also had a flash of realisation that the same terror of rejection ruled my relationship with Roger. There also seemed to be a strand which went further back (I later saw that this was to do with the issue of being rejected by my father). As well as all this, the very act of voicing the terror had a profound impact on my relationship with my counsellor. I felt much closer to him and much less scared when I realised that he was not going to turn me away as a hopeless case. This incident made it easier for me to tell him about my 'bridge' later in that meeting.

This incident seems to have contributed immeasurably to the trust between the counsellor and Joan, who was then able to share with him the details of her private suicide fantasy of jumping from a 'bridge' (see Chapter 7). The development of this significant trust is the point where we want to draw our arbitrary line to separate the 'beginning' and the 'middle' of the counselling process, because it is only when this trust develops that the client is prepared to take more risks in the relative certainty that the counsellor's acceptance and commitment will endure.

In this case trust has developed quite rapidly despite the counsellor's ineptitude at times. Two main factors contribute to the comparative speed of the process. Firstly, it is clear that Joan is in a high 'state of readiness' for counselling. Using the factors outlined earlier in this chapter (Box 6.2) as indicators of the client's state of readiness, it is clear that Joan was not dogged by indecision about wanting to change; that she did not suffer from a general lack of trust; that she was willing to take considerable responsibility for what happened in counselling; and that she was willing to recognise and explore her feelings. Where so many of these factors are present we would expect the beginning phase to be quite short. The counsellor also contributed to the speed of the process, because although he was in danger of over-identifying Joan with his other client, Christine, he was *aware* of that deficiency in himself and took care to *check* his perceptions of Joan. Although his was a clumsy beginning, the situation would only have been dangerous if he had been lacking in self-awareness or had been unwilling to check his assumptions.

The trust in the relationship between Joan and her counsellor has now been established to the extent that significant progress can be made. They have concluded the 'beginning' and are about to enter the 'middle' phase of their counselling process.

7

'Middles'

The Case-Study (Part 2)

Meeting 2 (continued)

Towards the end of this meeting came one of those moments in counselling when the client takes a great risk and finds that her trust has not
been misplaced. The quality of the counsellor's understanding established
a level of sharing which is the hallmark of *intimacy*. In the audio-tape of
the meeting there is a long silence, which is eventually broken by Joan:

JOAN [*lowers her head and speaks with a slow but firm voice*]:
  When I'm at my lowest I visit my 'bridge'. [*Pause*]. It's a high bridge
  over the railway. [*Pause*]. I do weird things like waiting for a train
  to come and then I imagine how my body would look if it was
  tumbling down towards the train – and I work out which carriage
  my body would hit . . . and how the pain would feel . . . and then
  the blackness . . . and nothingness. [*Pause*].
COUNSELLOR: It doesn't sound weird to me . . . it sounds very
  important – like it's very important for you?
JOAN: It is crucial for me – it is what keeps me sane – in fact it's what
  keeps me alive in a funny kind of way . . . [*pause*] I didn't think I
  would tell you about it because it's too important . . . too precious.
COUNSELLOR [*speaking slowly*]: Yes, I see that – I think I see just how
  precious it is – it's incredibly important to you – it is actually the

> means by which you are coping with your life . . . it is so so
> precious – I feel honoured that you have trusted me with it.
> Joan: [*smiles*].

The counsellor's understanding and acceptance in this exchange were experienced by Joan as offering a level of intimacy which added immeasurably to the strength of the relationship. Such intimate moments are never lost, as Joan commented two years later:

> This was a most beautiful moment – and amazing that it should
> happen as early as our second meeting. I trusted him enough to make
> him the only person in the world to know about my 'bridge'. And he
> understood so well its meaning and significance . . . and indeed its
> beauty for me. The only thing that I can remotely liken that experience
> to, is making love – sharing and treasuring together a very precious
> experience.

Meeting 3

The counsellor's notes explore the important elements for him in this third meeting.

> The *content* of this meeting is easy to describe. It was entirely devoted
> to Joan's growing feeling of disgust towards both her husband and
> herself in relation to the sado-masochistic practices in which they
> engaged. (Joan went into considerable detail on these practices and her
> feelings about them, past and present.) During this last week she has
> begun to refuse to take part in these activities.
> The *process* in the meeting seems to have been one of Joan 'unloading'
> some of the tension and guilt she feels about her SM sex – it seemed
> really important for her to tell me every bit of detail as though she was
> exorcising her guilt. It is also apparent that Joan is getting a little bit
> stronger already: I don't think that she could have refused her husband
> even two weeks ago . . . She's going very fast at present. But there was
> one strange thing about her today that I am only now aware of as I
> focus on her. I didn't really get the feeling that she was hugely disturbed
> by their sex life, and yet she seemed so very *intense* when she was telling
> me about it. Is there something else behind it that we missed? It's too
> late for now to do anything about it – to begin the next session with
> that would not be a good idea since it would pre-empt whatever is

important to her when she comes. But there does seem to be a difference in intensity between how she *was* in the session and what these practices *mean* for her. I shall store that up in case it arises in the future. Why did I miss this in the meeting itself? It seems so obvious now. I think I was a bit overawed by her SM experiences. I was blinded by them – I haven't had enough experience of the graphic details of SM – I was de-railed for a time and failed to sense the discrepancy between her content and her way of being.

Meeting 4

This extract from the counsellor's notes indicates the dominant theme of the fourth meeting.

Today Joan was as negative about herself and her situation as I have seen her since the first meeting. She repeated phrases like: 'It's no good'; 'I can't leave him', 'I'm no good – I'm powerless.'

This was one of those meetings where the unskilled helper might have tried to take Joan out of her mood of depression with some version of *'there, there now, it'll be alright'*. However, a more fruitful response is to see this depression and regression as an integral part of the client's process: sometimes clients have to experience their position at its worst before they can move on through it. The task of the person-centred counsellor is to be a companion on this part of the journey too, even though it is negative, depressing and at times irrational. Simply pointing out the irrationality of the regression does not stop it, and indeed can add to the client's experience of failure.

Twice during this meeting Joan said: 'I need to visit my bridge.' The counsellor went on to explore what that meant to her, but in doing that he later felt he had missed an opportunity, as he wrote in his notes:

I wish I had followed my intuition of suggesting that we might, literally, visit her bridge together. At the time I *knew* that that quick judgement of mine was soundly based and that I should follow it through. Our relationship is strong enough for her to have accepted me going with her to that most private place. Being with her there might have helped to loosen her present 'stuckness'.

The person-centred counsellor should not feel confined to the physical boundaries of the counselling office. That room serves as a meeting place because it is convenient and private: sometimes these advantages are worth sacrificing for other benefits which might follow. Accompanying the client to her 'bridge' might have been a way of pursuing the issues that were important to her, but in a place which was more powerfully evocative.

Meeting 5

This meeting opened with the counsellor's question: 'What is happening for you this week?', to which Joan replied: 'Nothing very much'. Joan appeared very quiet and withdrawn during the first third of the meeting. The counsellor eventually confronted this quietness and Joan's avoidance of eye contact, by being open about his experience of these:

COUNSELLOR: It feels that you've been avoiding looking at me today . . . and you seem much quieter . . . how are you feeling?

JOAN: [*bursts into tears*] It's so hopeless – I'm hopeless – I can't do it – I just can't leave him [Roger].

COUNSELLOR: Is there any other feeling there as well?'

JOAN: I'm hopeless . . . [*pause*] I feel that I'm letting you down.

COUNSELLOR: Letting me down because you're not as strong as you have been?

JOAN: Yes, I'm so embarrassed.

COUNSELLOR: As though I'm probably not going to like you very much when you are this way?

JOAN: [*still avoiding eye contact*] No – how could anyone like a crying little girl? [*She pulls her legs up under her on the seat and holds them with her arms, burying her head in her knees. Her crying becomes a deep sobbing.*]

COUNSELLOR: [*moves from his seat to sit beside Joan on the couch and gently puts his arm around her. They stay like that for nearly five minutes with Joan sobbing continuously.*]

For the remainder of the meeting the counsellor sat beside Joan who, once she had stopped sobbing, began to talk about the continual sadness she had felt in her life as a young girl.

The counsellor in this extract operated very fully as a person-centred practitioner. He was not only accurately empathic in relation to Joan's deepening unhappiness, indeed desolation, but he showed a consistently high valuing of Joan even while she was behaving in ways which *she* felt would be unacceptable. In all of this the counsellor was perfectly congruent with the quality and intensity of his own feelings and sensations; he was even willing to show the fullness of his response to Joan by moving towards her and holding her while she cried.

It might be difficult to judge the importance of an interaction like this without being in the situation. Joan was very clear on her view of the counsellor's behaviour in her later reflections:

> It felt that he was willing to just *be with me* in my hopelessness and depression. He didn't try to take me out of it. That felt most important although it is difficult to describe why it was important. It is something to do with the fact that at the very time I expected him to *reject* me he actually came *towards* me and sat beside me – that meant that he really, genuinely was with me, and I could then face the full intensity of my desolation and somehow get through it.

The counsellor gives a similar view of this interaction in his notes:

> Today was a critical session for Joan and also for our relationship. I was able to meet her on her very desolate ground, and share that with her. She certainly was going through powerful feelings, because the sensations which I experienced were incredibly charged: I was tingling with the sensation of her desperation and sadness. I could feel her with my whole body, and at the end of the session I felt both exhausted and enervated.

Meeting 6

Joan arrived ten minutes early and since the counsellor was ready, the meeting began. Without waiting for an invitation, Joan started recounting the various half-forgotten memories and thoughts which had come flooding into her consciousness during the past week. She spoke at length of the hitherto unmentioned fact that her father had regularly used her for sexual intercourse when she was aged between thirteen and sixteen. Sometimes the sexual intercourse would be preceded by various acts of physical cruelty. She spoke of these activities in just as much detail as she had earlier devoted to her sado-masochistic relationship with her husband. While speaking, she shook constantly, sometimes with 'hate', but also 'anger', 'fear', and later with 'desperation'. Near the end of the session she summed up her position with the rhetorical question: 'What do I do with all this feeling?'

As well as speaking of her father's cruelty Joan was bitter about the role which her mother had played. The following extract from one of Joan's monologues sums this up:

> I kept quiet about it just like daddy said for ages and ages, but I kept hoping that mummy would find out. One time I thought she *must* have found out when she came in early and found me crying on the bed. I felt so bad – more than anything else I felt so guilty that she had found out – but I *wanted* her to find out. She left my room without a word and went downstairs. I kept waiting for her to come up again but she never did and I fell asleep. The next day she acted like nothing had happened – and so did I.
>
> Looking back on it now I am absolutely sure that she knew what was going on, but she covered it up . . . and she didn't help me. Shortly after that time my father stopped doing it, and I was left totally alone. I remember feeling that I wanted to be dead all over because I had caused such terrible things to my daddy and mummy.

In the same meeting Joan made the connection between her relations with her father and those with her husband: 'it was almost as though I was picking another daddy and trying to get it right this time'. When the counsellor reflected on the apparent similarity in the sensations she seemed to experience as a sixteen-year-old 'wanting to be dead all over' and the 'blackness' and 'nothingness' which she found in her fantasy of jumping from the bridge, Joan recognised the parallels and went on to focus upon the other sensations, as well as 'comfort', which went along with this fantasy retreat into annihilation.

This meeting also highlighted a change in her relationship with Roger. As well as uncovering some of her reasons for picking him as a partner, she reported that in the previous week she had been able to tell him about the incest. She had cried a lot with him and he had responded better than she had expected: 'He didn't seem to know what was going on, but at least he held me and patted me – he showed as much concern as he could.'

In the account of this meeting we have not said very much about the behaviour of the counsellor. The truth of the matter is that it was the counsellor's behaviour in the *previous* session which facilitated the awakening of Joan's memories and her account of these in the present meeting. During the sixth meeting the counsellor had very little to do; at this point in the counselling process the client was entirely in charge of her own process. The presence of the counsellor is important, but what he does is becoming less crucial since the client is more able to take responsibility for herself. Their relationship is moving towards a state of '*mutuality*'.

Meetings 7, 8 and 9

Probably the most difficult thing to predict in the counselling process is its speed. Sometimes clients start slowly and later go very fast, while at other times the start is fast, only to be followed by a lull. As it transpired, the latter pattern fitted our present case. During meetings 7, 8 and 9 Joan faced and re-faced the material which had been generated between meetings 5 and 6. She went round the issues time and time again, processing and re-processing. This kind of apparently 'stuck' phase in a counselling process can be difficult for the counsellor. When it seems to persist, meeting after meeting, the patience of the counsellor is tested to the extreme. And yet such phases are often important facets of the client's process – it takes more than a few hours to change one's life. In Joan's case she had discovered much more than she had expected by the end of meeting 6. In a sense things had gone almost too fast for her in that time, and it is not surprising that it took her a few weeks to 'catch up' on herself. Two years later Joan was able to reflect on this phase of the counselling process:

About the middle of our time together we went round in circles for
quite a long time. It seemed that neither of us knew where to go next –
and everything we tried drew a blank. I now realise that I was stuck
because at some level I realised the enormity of what I had uncovered.
I had come into counselling apparently hoping for help in making
some changes in my present life, and suddenly I was coming to terms
with the fact that my father used to torture me, then screw me, that my
mother secretly colluded in all our denial of that and that I had
married my husband because he was sexually cruel like my father!

Some extracts from the counsellor's notes show how difficult this phase can be, and how the person-centred counsellor will be concerned to try to detect the *locus* of the stuckness. If it is in the *client* then patient attention is likely to bring reward, but if the locus of stuckness is either in the *counsellor* or in their *relationship,* then more direct action is required of the counsellor:

As I suspected, we really do now seem to be well and truly stuck. I am convinced that the stuckness does not have to do with our relationship. Certainly our relationship is not stuck through lack of involvement. Also I don't think the stuckness is coming from me. I get no sense of withholding myself which would normally create stuckness. Nor do I feel that Joan is threatening any of my values which might cause me to become inhibiting towards her. I am aware that I am not surprised by her stuckness – perhaps I even expected it a little bit. When she came out with that mountain of stuff in our sixth meeting I remember thinking that she would take some time to process all that. I really do think that this is Joan's stuckness without pollution from myself. She seems blocked in herself, as she said today: 'I feel I am choking inside . . . I feel I am stifling myself.'

As I am sitting focusing on it, I think that although I have not been creating the stuckness, I may actually have been contributing to it. I have felt so frustrated and I realise there have been a number of occasions when I have tried to help Joan find ways out of her stuckness. What I might do instead is to really try and *accept her in her stuckness* (if it persists). Just as with all her other feelings I will try to get right into it with her – and be stuck together. That way I will be available to her in her own efforts to find a way out. Why didn't I see this earlier – I can be so stupid!

Meeting 10

When the person-centred counsellor uncovers, between meetings, a possible avenue for exploration, he would not normally *begin* the next session with this. Instead he would start with whatever was most prominent for the client and use the time to check on the persistency of his reaction to what was happening. In this particular case the counsellor waited some twenty minutes during which Joan seemed to be going over old ground, before he intervened to give his reactions as accurately and as fully as he could:

I'm feeling pretty stuck – I've had this feeling on and off in our last few meetings. It's a funny feeling, because I feel OK about what we're doing and what we've done together. But after last week's meeting I realised that I hadn't really been listening to what was happening in you. I had got used to you steaming along like an express train and I seemed to be looking for ways of pushing you on and on. But I think I failed to realise that your express train has stopped in the station for the time being and that maybe we might look at what that means.

In this statement the counsellor is being absolutely congruent in his response to Joan. Congruent responses are sometimes quite lengthy, with the counsellor taking care to represent accurately, not just his dominant reaction in relation to his client, but all the details of that response.

Although the counsellor's response was emphasising his impression that Joan was temporarily stuck, paradoxically it had the opposite effect of helping her to experience her present feelings more intensely and thereafter to move on. One of the marvels of human relationships is that if a helper tries to pull a client out of her feeling this often results in the client being stuck with it, while the alternative approach of endeavouring to understand and fully appreciate the client's experience frequently results in an intensification of the experience which is then the prelude to subsequent movement. One of the distinctive features of the person-centred approach is its capacity to capitalise on this process.

In focusing on her feelings about her history, anger first became prominent for Joan. While she was expressing her anger by screaming, she began to cry and slumped off her chair to squat on the floor. Her crying eventually changed to a deep sobbing and at that point the counsellor left his own chair to squat with her, still facing her. The counsellor takes up the account, not from his notes, but from memory two years later, prompted by the audio-tape of the meeting:

> I kept expecting her to stop, but she went on and on and eventually I
> realised that this sobbing came from the very kernel of her existence.
> This was sobbing which had been stored up for many years. As I sat
> with her I sensed that she was allowing that abused 'little girl' inside her
> to see the light of day and to do what had been forbidden many years
> before – to cry for herself. I remember thinking at the time that
> perhaps this was another beginning; the beginning of what would
> become her self-acceptance.

Joan also helps us to understand the process as she experienced it with this comment two years later:

> I think what happened was that very early in our meetings I opened the
> door to my feelings. A little came out, although it felt like a lot at the
> time, and then in terror at just how much feeling there was, I closed the

door. I didn't do it consciously, it was as though at some level I knew I couldn't take it and my defences closed the door to my experience of the anger and most especially of the deep deep sadness at what my mother and father had done. I had been scared at the beginning, then I got less scared and some feeling came out, but then my fear returned. Only in this tenth meeting did my feelings fully uncork.

Meetings 11 to 14

Unfortunately, laziness on the part of the counsellor resulted in an almost total absence of notes following these sessions, so we have to rely on information from the audio-tapes along with the reflections of Joan and the counsellor some two years later. Joan begins by commenting on what happened to her after meeting 10:

> Once I had really opened up my anger and my sadness, they didn't just come out and then go away. They came back time and time again, but each time it was a little bit less. Even now I get angry and sad about it, and I guess I always will. But from that point onwards a lot of things changed quite suddenly. Well, it wasn't so much outside things which changed, but it was my way of looking at them that was different. Roger was no longer the ogre who totally dominated my existence. Instead he was a rather weak guy who had his own problems. I knew now that I *could* leave him. Funnily enough that made me less desperate to leave though I knew it would happen when the time was right.
> Listening to the tapes it is really obvious how my voice has changed in these sessions [11–14]. From being squeaky, brittle, and excited, it has become stable, calm, and mature. I have come out of my 'lost little girl' and suddenly I am able to be the woman who has choices in her life.

Joan's comment sums up quite well her state of being in these sessions. The issues to which she was attending centred on her taking control of her life. She knew that she had married Roger largely because he was similar to her father, and that their SM practices also reflected her relationship with her father, as she said in one session:

> My aim in life became to have Roger love me while hurting me – unlike my daddy who had sex with me, and hurt me, but whom I felt never really loved me.

Her growing awareness of herself also uncovered the fact that she had behaved seductively towards most of her bosses, and had quite deliberately hidden her intellectual ability in previous jobs. She felt that this was all part of the pattern in which she repeatedly confirmed herself as 'an inadequate little girl'.

The 'end of the middle' of the therapeutic process comes during sessions 11–14, where it is clear that Joan has largely faced and overcome the emotional blockages which have been inhibiting the process of her life; she has begun to achieve self-acceptance, and she can now be freer to make changes in her life.

Our discussion of meetings 11–14 continues at the beginning of Chapter 8, as Joan and her counsellor move through the final period of their counselling process. There are, however, a number of general issues which warrant discussion before we leave this middle part of the therapeutic process, and to these we now turn.

'MIDDLES' – AN OVERVIEW

The person-centred counsellor does not conceptualise her work as following a clearly definable series of steps. Instead she recognises that each client is unique, and that the therapeutic process which he experiences will be different from that of any other individual. This emphasis on the uniqueness of each client does not mean, however, that it is meaningless to investigate the counselling process. There are some issues – the establishing of *trust*, for example – which are so fundamental that they will play a major part in work with every client, and there are other processes which, although they may not be important in every counselling contact, are still distinctive and central to the person-centred approach. The sharing of *intimacy*, the development of *mutuality* and the client's *achievement of self-acceptance* are three such processes which are often crucial in the middle period. Furthermore there are some events which only occasionally occur within a therapeutic process but nonetheless warrant examination because they can present profound problems if the counsellor is not aware of their importance. This last group includes *stuckness* and the question of the boundary between the counsellor's full therapeutic involvement and her *over-involvement*. The remainder of this chapter will explore all these aspects of the counselling process.

The counsellor in the case-study paid attention to three dimensions: the development of the therapeutic relationship, the client's process and the counsellor's process. We shall consider the issues relevant to this middle period of the therapeutic process under the same three headings.

THE DEVELOPMENT OF THE THERAPEUTIC RELATIONSHIP

The development of a significant degree of *trust* between client and counsellor was a crucial part of the 'beginning' of the counselling process, but this does not mean that trust ceases to be an important issue as the relationship continues. We would expect trust to deepen and to be reinforced as counsellor and client learn more about each other. Nor is it a one-way process: the counsellor comes to trust the client as much as the client the counsellor. This aspect of trust has received little attention in the literature and research on counselling, and yet from the clinical reports of counsellors in supervision, the extent to which they trust the client has a significant part to play in the development of the therapeutic relationship. The same social and emotional difficulties which can block the counsellor's empathy, acceptance or congruence can similarly make it more difficult for the counsellor to trust her client. Parodoxically the counsellor is often helped by the client whose developing trust in the counselling process makes it easier for the counsellor to trust him. In our case-study Joan was quite ready to trust the counsellor. In many ways she was much more centred at the beginning than was the counsellor. It took only some understanding and intimate contact in the second meeting to make Joan sure of her trust, and in turn this helped the counsellor to be more open, understanding and caring towards her. As the therapeutic relationship develops, trust between counsellor and client spirals onwards: the more one of them trusts and is open with the other, then the easier it is for the other to respond with similar trust and openness. This reciprocal trust leads directly to the development of *mutuality* which will be discussed later.

Another experience which can contribute to the development of mutuality in the therapeutic relationship is *intimacy.* There are several examples of intimate moments between counsellors and clients in this book. Many of these correspond to times when the client experiences the counsellor as showing complete understanding and valuing. In our case-study there are such intimate moments in meeting 2 when Joan took the risk of speaking of her fear of rejection and again when they shared the importance which Joan's 'bridge' played in her life. In meeting 5 when, in Joan's words, the counsellor was 'willing to just be with me in my hopelessness and depression' we see a similar moment of intimacy. At times such as these, understanding between client and counsellor exists at many levels, as does acceptance. The outcome is a profound sense of sharing. Such moments, which can be marked simply by a gentle touch, a brief reciprocated glance, or even just sitting silently together, tend to stand out and to be remembered by both client and counsellor long afterwards. For the client whose history of relationships has been disturbed and whose self-acceptance is weak, such intimacy may be a unique experience and is therefore powerfully instrumental in the development of his self-regard.

The establishment of *mutuality* is a central process as the therapeutic relationship develops during person-centred counselling. From the time when mutuality is established, both counsellor and client experience their work as a truly shared enterprise and they can trust each other's commitment to achieve and maintain genuineness in relation to each other. Neither is fearful of the other, and intimacy comes easily in ways which are appropriate to the counselling setting. The various forms of human defensiveness which characterise everyday relationships are largely absent between the counsellor and client who have developed mutuality – they have nothing to fear in each other in the counselling context. Increasingly they become so transparent that they can no longer be symbols for each other but can dare to see each other clearly. The counsellor now has no difficulty in releasing her empathic sensitivity in whatever ways are most congruent to her. The client, too, becomes more active in making suggestions as to how they might proceed – and he might even make rather unusual requests of the counsellor in the certain trust that the counsellor will respond honestly. (For instance, at the end of our case-study, Joan makes the unexpected request that the counsellor accompany her on a visit to her mother's grave.)

The establishment of mutuality is important in other ways. It can be the time when the client moves from being nourished by the counsellor's acceptance to being able to replace that with his own developing self-acceptance. This is not to say that the counsellor stops showing her esteem for the client, but that for the client increasing importance attaches to his ability to value himself and to trust that inner process: his *locus of evaluation* in the relationship has moved from the counsellor to himself. Such a shift is certainly apparent in our case-study where meeting 10 seems to be the focal point by which time mutuality is established. After that time Joan's whole attitude and approach to her life have changed: she is clearer about the value of aspects of her life, like her marriage; she has greater certainty about her own value; and she is able to be much more effective in initiating change in her life where that is necessary. From this point onwards her *need for the counsellor* is much less central, though her valuing of him is still high. Once mutuality is established, progress is usually fast: having experienced himself as capable of relating to another human being openly and without fear, the client knows that he can indeed relate differently to other people in his life. Gradually he can move towards being similarly self-accepting and congruent in relation to others outside the counselling relationship.

We have emphasised the notion of 'mutuality' because it is a common development in person-centred counselling. However, this does not mean that such a state occurs in *every* counselling relationship. There are times when the therapeutic relationship does not develop in this way, and where the client chooses, for whatever reason, to keep the counsellor at arm's length. Such relationships can still be both warm and productive.

THE CLIENT'S PROCESS

In a video-taped interview shortly before his death, Carl Rogers said: 'There are some very special moments in a person's life when they feel able to change. Hopefully more of these happen in therapy' (Bennis, 1986). This is in fact a very simple statement of what person-centred counselling aims to do: it seeks to create more of those 'special moments' when the client will feel able to change.

Essentially person-centred counselling endeavours to create such moments by *freeing the natural healing process within the client*. As discussed more fully in Chapter 1, the person-centred approach assumes that people basically want to be 'healthy' in the psychological as well as the physical sense, and that they have the potential to develop such positive mental health. The task of the counsellor, through the counselling relationship, is to help the client to free that process – so that he can gradually lay aside the various things which inhibit or totally block this healing process. Social and emotional isolation, fear, denial, lack of clarity, lack of awareness of feelings, paralysing self-doubt and self-rejection are typical examples of such blocks. Through the relationship which the counsellor creates, the client is no longer so isolated socially and emotionally, and his fear diminishes as his trust increases, for fear and trust are opposite sides of the same coin. This reduction in fear is the key which unlocks other doors; when the client is not so fearful he can face the difficulties which up till then he has had to deny. The world of his feelings becomes less threatening and more accessible to him. Experiencing a relationship with the counsellor where he is deeply valued makes it increasingly difficult for him to deny his own value, and begins the disintegration of the barrier of self-doubt or self-rejection. This gradual freeing of the healing process within the client, sometimes called *movement* in counselling, is beautifully described by Goff Barrett-Lennard (1987) as 'the passage from wound-edness to hope'.

It is interesting to reflect more closely on what actually happens when a client 'changes' in a therapeutic process. We tend to use that word 'change' rather glibly without really considering what it means. In another book, Mearns refers to '*seismic*' change and exemplifies that with this case study of 'Joan'

> it is as though the pressure towards change has been building up under the surface and then quite suddenly a major shift takes place. (1994: 92)

This can be compared to '*osmotic*' change, described thus:

> In this form of change it is as though the client has not been aware of the self-concept change which has slowly developed. The process has taken place so gradually that each element of the change was imperceptible, but there has come a time when the client notices the effects of the accumulated change. (Mearns, 1994: 92)

In 'osmotic' change the counsellor may have been seeing the change long before the client. The experience is encapsulated by one client as: '*It feels really strange . . . nothing has changed, yet everything is different*'.

One of the interesting aspects of what we call 'change' is that the client is not left with something entirely new and unfamiliar. He does not have to start afresh and work out how to operate this 'changed' Self. In fact, quite the opposite is true. Although the client may feel somewhat unfamiliar with matters such as the gain in confidence and reduced defensiveness, he operates rather fluidly and proficiently and not at all like someone learning anew. Perhaps it is not that the Self has 'changed', but that the interrelationship of 'configurations' within the Self has altered (Mearns, 1998a). In this conception the Self is comprised of a number of 'parts' or 'configurations' interrelating like a family, with an individual variety of dynamics. When the interrelationship of configurations changes, it is not that we are left with something entirely new: we have the same 'parts' as before, but some which may have been sub-servient before are stronger, others which were judged adversely are accepted, some which were in self-negating conflict have come to respect each other, and overall the parts have achieved constructive integration with the energy release which arises from such fusion. Carl Rogers added little to his theory of Self after 1963 (Mearns, 1997a), but we are now at a very exciting time in person-centred theory when we are seeking to develop that theory and empirically test the hypotheses which arise (Mearns, 1998a).

Since movement in person-centred counselling depends upon the removal of blockages such as those mentioned earlier, it is unlikely to be an even and regular process. The trainee counsellor can be grossly misled by writers and trainers who over-simplify the process into a series of neat and ordered stages. Such 'stages' present the trainee with the welcome illusion of an understandable and predictable process. But it is a fiction and one which leads the trainee away from the central activity of tracking the client. Once the trainee is expecting, and waiting for, the client to follow a pattern which has been laid down for him by the theoreticians he has abandoned the person-centred perspective.

The experienced person-centred counsellor knows and feels comfortable with the fact that her client's movement is likely to include periods of stuckness or regression and that there will be many plateaux and lulls. Furthermore, the counsellor will know that most often these apparent 'hiccups' are natural aspects of the freeing of the client's healing process. Such phases are often indicative of the fact that the client needs to gain further strength before moving on, and they require the counsellor's attentive companionship just as much as times of rapid movement or dramatic change.

With movement in person-centred counselling being such an individual process, it is not easy for the counsellor to be certain about what is happening at any particular moment. Her *faith in the process* can help to sustain her through such uncertainty. This simply means an affirmation of her firm belief that if she can consistently offer the therapeutic conditions as fully as possible, then although the movement may be erratic and seem to get stuck at times, the overall direction and effect will be positive. This is one reason why inexperienced person-centred counsellors need to be supervised by practitioners from the same tradition, for it can sometimes be difficult to trust the process when that process has all the appearance of having ground to a halt. A supervisor from another school of thought might inappropriately panic and encourage the counsellor to push the client at precisely the wrong juncture.

Experienced counsellors are well aware that clients often *appear to get*

148

worse before they get better, but this too can be difficult for the new practitioner who may be confused when she sees her client apparently
deteriorate despite what seems to her to be a good working relationship.
One way of understanding this phenomenon is to remember that before
he seeks professional help the client will have been coping as best as he can
by defending himself against his difficulties. He may have denied many of
his fearful feelings, tried to avoid situations which would arouse his sadness or anger, restricted his way of relating with others to minimise
emotional contact and risk – in short he will have constructed many bar-
riers to protect himself. As the counselling process begins and the client's
fear diminishes he will begin to take more risks by facing situations which
he might previously have avoided, and by being open to feelings of which
he had earlier been afraid. To those around him, he may cause distress by
breaking down and crying more often, or showing the anger which was
earlier suppressed, or becoming very emotionally needy or demanding. In
that beautiful and ageless book by Virginia Axline, devoted entirely to the
case-study of her play therapy work with one six-year-old boy, Dibs
(Axline, 1971), we see that when Dibs really began to make progress in
therapy he appeared to his parents to be 'more disturbed'. He was in fact
feeling stronger and more able to show his anger and his sadness, whereas
previously he had suppressed these. In our own case-study Joan shows
some strength after the second meeting as she begins to initiate changes at
home, but by the fourth and fifth meetings she has apparently slumped
down into profound feelings of powerlessness and negativity. We see later,
in meetings 5 and 6, however, that it has been of crucial importance for
Joan to have got to the bottom of her pit of desolation and to share that
with the counsellor. She had been able to experience fully the deep desperation she had known as a young girl. Previously it had never been safe
enough to allow that feeling into full awareness, and the result was that
she had always been blocked by it. An important part of the healing
process which is released in the client is that he begins to 'accept himself'
in the sense that he starts to cherish himself as a person of worth; a
person who assuredly has weaknesses and strengths, but one who is fundamentally of value.

A number of factors in the person-centred relationship contribute to
the development of *self-acceptance*, including the counsellor's consistent
acceptance (see Chapter 4), and the releasing of emotional blocks which
have locked the client, perhaps for years, in a negative view of himself – in
Joan's case, for example, she was released from the fear and guilt associated with her abuse as a child. Sometimes it is awe-inspiring how rapidly

a client can move from the pit of depression to a state of basic self-acceptance in which everything seems different. As we shall see in the next chapter on endings, the client may still have much to do to reshape his life, but when the core of self-acceptance is established the most important part of the counselling work is accomplished and the change for the client is *irreversible*. One client described how this emerging self-acceptance felt:

> It feels as though nothing has changed, but everything has changed. I came into counselling thinking that what I wanted to do was to make a number of changes in my life. So far I haven't made any changes in my life, and my whole life has changed. The change has happened to *me*: for the first time in my life I can say that I have good points and bad points, but basically I am OK as a human being. Although nothing else in my outside life has changed, this will change it all: this will allow me to be loving as a partner, it will allow me to show my love to my children; it will allow me to look at the work I do and decide what parts I want to keep, and it will allow me to meet people and not be afraid of them.

This achievement of basic self-acceptance is usually followed by a sharp increase in the client's *personal power*. Analogies with physics are more poetic than scientific, but it is as though the fusion within the person through his self-acceptance releases a huge amount of energy. This is just as well, because once self-acceptance is established a client often wishes to make many changes in his life, as we shall see in Chapter 8, and he will need all the energy he can command to be able to do this.

THE COUNSELLOR'S PROCESS

The person-centred counsellor also goes through a process during the course of the counselling relationship. Once trust is established the counsellor is just as relieved as the client, and in much the same way as the client she then finds it easier to become more *fully involved* in the therapeutic relationship. The freedom which trust brings makes it easier for the counsellor to risk more of her own congruent reactions to the client. Now she is really able to offer herself as a mirror to her client and utilise the full potential of her congruence, as detailed in Chapter 5. In our case-study we note the counsellor doing this as early as meeting 3. In reflecting on that meeting afterwards he drew on his own felt sense of the client in coming to the hypothesis that there might be more behind Joan's feelings about her husband and their SM practices. There was no adequate space to make use of this hypothesis at that time, but its validity was later realised when Joan's abuse emerged. Similarly, in meeting 5, when the counsellor sat beside Joan, he was able to tap his own bodily sensations as a reflection of her experience: 'I was tingling with the sensation of her desperation. I could feel her with my whole body'. Another clear example came in meeting 10 when the counsellor squatted in front of Joan on the floor and for the first time really felt the depth of her sadness. There were many other examples of the counsellor's use of his self in relation to Joan, but these were among the most striking in our case-study notes.

In exploring the full involvement of the counsellor in the counselling process we must address the question of the difference between such full involvement and *over-involvement*. Like most other counselling practitioners we recognise the counsellor's 'over-involvement' as damaging to the therapeutic process, as well as sometimes being unethical. Indeed, because such a high degree of personal involvement is required of the person-centred counsellor, over-involvement is regarded even more seriously because it threatens the very basis of person-centred work by undermining the client's trust in the integrity and professionalism of the counsellor. When that trust is abused by a counsellor it damages not only the therapeutic relationship in question, but the integrity of the whole approach and its underlying rationale.

Over-involvement is more easily recognised than defined, but the following might serve as a crude guideline:

'Over-involvement' exists when meeting the counsellor's emotional needs or wishes has become of equal or greater concern than meeting those of the client.

It must be recognised that in the course of her work with clients the counsellor will often be having some of her needs or wishes met. If this were not the case then it is difficult to see what would motivate the counsellor to continue in the profession. In the main these will be needs or wishes which are compatible with the role of professional counsellor. For instance, they might include: a wish to offer help to others; a need to function in a professional way; a wish to maintain integrity; a wish to experience meaningful/close communication with others; and an emotional as well as practical need to be financially rewarded for her work.

Over-involvement takes different forms depending on the emotional needs or wishes which the counsellor is principally concerned to have met. A common form is where the counsellor uses her relationship with the client as a means of confirming her own importance by exerting power over others. The person-centred approach is not the most fertile ground for the power-oriented counsellor who might be more attracted to more counsellor-centred approaches. But in the context of the person-centred approach the symptoms of this abuse of power might include the creation of excessive dependency among her clients; repeated and strong instances of unresolved feelings of love and/or hate; and a failure ever to reach a state of mutuality with the client.

A counsellor who seeks sexual gratification with a client is unquestionably over-involved and, regardless of the intricacies of the client's or her own motivation, is deemed to be behaving unethically. There are no exceptions or qualifications. Even when the person-centred counsellor reaches a state of mutuality with the client, whereby power is equally shared in the relationship, the counsellor remains professionally responsible to the client and this precludes sexual relations.

Having stressed the dangers of over-involvement, and particularly of sexual relations, while having earlier in this chapter placed great value on intimacy in the therapeutic relationship, we cannot fail to address the important question of what place, if any, the counsellor's *sexuality* can have in the therapeutic relationship.

Texts on counselling usually ignore the issue of sexuality completely. However, we consider it extremely important for the counsellor to come to recognise, understand, and feel comfortable with her sexuality. Counsellors should know that at times they may find that their strong positive feeling for a client has that same edge and quality as a loving response to a sexual partner. Sexuality is a normal part of human responsiveness and as such there will be occasions when the counsellor will recognise sexual feelings as an aspect of her attraction to the client.

The counsellor's sexuality carries danger only if she *over-reacts* to it in any of the following three ways:

1 if the counsellor engages in sexual activity with her client;
2 if the counsellor, unaware of her attraction, sends sexual *signals* to the client;
3 if the counsellor reacts to her own sexuality by *rejecting* the client: often this would take the form of the counsellor becoming a little colder or withdrawing slightly from the client, without explanation. This is one of the more common reactions to sexual feelings, and might

be disturbing to the client for whom issues of acceptance and rejection are critical.

Sexuality is a normal part of being human. Far from pretending that sexuality does not exist, we would encourage person-centred counsellors to reflect upon and discuss the issue of their sexuality, and for this to be a particular focus of attention in training and supervision. Sexuality becomes less threatening when it does not have to be denied and when the counsellor is confident in the knowledge that she will not exploit a client for her own sexual gratification.

Before concluding our discussion of the counsellor's process we want to emphasise the importance of the counsellor *making mistakes.* To the new counsellor, books like this can seem intimidating because the practitioners producing them seem to know exactly what is happening in the process of counselling, and seldom seem to make mistakes. We have tried to shake that myth a little by retaining examples which include what might commonly be called mistakes, or very untidy work, as in the early stages of our case-study where the counsellor's attention to Joan was contaminated by his experience with another client. Making mistakes is part of the process of counselling. In Chapter 3 on empathy there were a number of examples where the counsellor was not completely accurate in her understanding of the client, but her genuine attempts, even if they were wrong, were corrected by the client and the understanding of both improved. In general terms the same applies to the whole process of person-centred counselling: at times the counsellor will make mistakes, but unless she is over-dominant in the relationship the client will feel the freedom and the power to correct them. New practitioners can be afraid of their power in the counselling relationship and may feel that if they do anything wrong it will profoundly damage the client. In fact, clients are not so easily damaged – a client who has had considerable trouble in his life is likely to have developed quite sophisticated defences which he can also use to protect himself from the erring counsellor. The counsellor's mistakes may waste the client's time, but unless they are malevolently intended they seldom result in lasting damage.

'STUCKNESS' IN THE THERAPEUTIC PROCESS

The following five questions can be asked by the counsellor who is exploring an apparent phase of stuckness in the therapeutic process:

1 Are we indeed stuck, or am I misperceiving the process through my own impatience, or perhaps because I expect the client to move in a different direction from what is happening just now?
2 How does my client perceive the process at this time?
   If we *are* stuck:
3 What is the *source* of our stuckness?
4 How far is it important to our process at this time that we are stuck?
5 How might we move on?

Once the existence of stuckness is recognised and acknowledged by both counsellor and client, the key question in the series becomes the third: 'what is the *source* of our stuckness?' Finding the source of the stuckness makes it possible to answer question 4 on its importance to the therapeutic process, and also opens up likely answers to question 5 on how the process might move on.

There are three possible sources of stuckness in the counselling process: the *client,* the *counsellor,* or the *relationship* between client and counsellor. These can occur separately or in combination.

One example of stuckness primarily emanating from the *client* is where he seems to move a little way in counselling and then gets stuck at a point when he feels he has gained something, and is reluctant to risk that progress by going further. There is also the client whose exceptional ability to tolerate the most traumatic circumstances and emotions actually contrives to stop him from progressing – such a client will have defences so well developed that he can deny or minimise the desperation which for another client would be the motivator for change.

Sometimes the client gets temporarily stuck because his earlier movement has been so rapid and profound. It is as though so much progress has been made that he has to 'pause' in order to catch up with himself. This was particularly apparent in the phase of stuckness which took place during meetings 3, 4 and 5 in our case-study. It was also an aspect of the stuckness in meetings 7, 8 and 9, but during that latter phase a further factor was involved – namely Joan's realisation that her future seemed full of impossible choices. Again this is a common source of stuckness: the client has experienced a significant movement in counselling and realises that there is no going back, but to go on may lead to considerable life changes. It is scarcely surprising that the client in such a situation may pause to gather energy and coherence for the difficulties which lie ahead.

It is important that the person-centred counsellor is sensitive to the client's stuckness, and recognises that in many cases it is highly appropriate to the client's therapeutic process. It is easy for counsellors to 'make things happen' in counselling. Some other counselling approaches have a plethora of cathartic exercises which are often very attractive to counsellors who are looking for dramatic action. But it is important for the person-centred counsellor to recognise that *all* aspects of the therapeutic process are important: in the longer term, dramatic 'discoveries' are useful only in so far as the client can integrate them and integration often takes longer than discovery. In our case-study almost every major 'discovery' which Joan made was followed by a pause or a period of stuckness while adjustment and integration took place.

Stuckness in the therapeutic process can also originate in the *counsellor*. For instance, just as the client can settle for partial success rather than risk going further, sometimes the counsellor behaves in the same way. Perhaps she feels that she is doing a good job if she simply helps the client to cope with his present difficulties without further disturbing his life situation, so counselling proceeds with a lack of any kind of challenge which could move it on.

If the counsellor is fearful of being fully present in the counselling relationship it is unlikely that the therapeutic process will reach the stage of mutuality; indeed the counsellor's fear of being fully present is a 'super-glue' to the therapeutic process which can stick it at any point. When the counsellor cannot be fully present, then the power of the relationship can never be fully harnessed.

The counsellor's stuckness in relation to a facet of her own life might well result in the client becoming stuck on a similar issue. For instance, if the counsellor has not successfully negotiated a transition, then it can be difficult for her to help her client to negotiate the same transition. The client may get stuck at the same point; for instance, not being able to get beyond being angry at the spouse who left, or continuing to feel guilty about being sexually abused, or not being able to face the full extent of grief over a lost child.

Our third potential source of stuckness is the *relationship* between counsellor and client. This stuckness takes the form of *restrictive patterns* which develop in the relationship. Both client and counsellor may feel that the process is going well, but in fact they can be secretly colluding in ways which make it less effective. Perhaps they are stuck in a pattern of the client being weak and the counsellor being powerful, or maybe the pattern is one where they are both locked into focusing only on possible solutions to immediate difficulties; or the pattern could involve the avoidance of intense feeling and a reliance on simply *thinking* about the client's problems. There are countless patterns in relationships, and they can be difficult to identify and unravel. The exercise reproduced in Chapter 3 as Box 3.6 can be helpful in identifying patterns, and of course the most useful person here is the counsellor's supervisor who may be the first to identify and challenge such stuckness in the relationship. Even then, the supervisor may only identify it from *audio-tapes* of the counsellor's work.

One way in which the therapeutic process can become 'stuck' is if the people concerned do not know when and how to bring their relationship to a close. We shall now return to our case-study to see that, when the client is able to accept herself and face the feelings which she most feared, then she is freer to make changes in her life and the counselling process can move towards its ending.

8

'ENDINGS'

THE CASE-STUDY (PART 3)

Meetings 11–14 (continued)

In these four meetings Joan reviewed her professional life and determined to resume the studies which she had previously dropped upon protestations from Roger. She also started dancing classes for the first time since she was fourteen years old, and arranged a holiday with a female friend. She felt sorry for Roger but not regretful about the fact that emotionally at least she had deserted him (although she was very shaken when he threatened suicide).

It soon became apparent that, once freed of the fear of feeling her own anger and sadness, Joan was able to internalise her *locus of evaluation* (see Chapter 1). It was clear, too, that she was building up her self-esteem faster than would usually happen in a person who had earlier arrived at such a profoundly negative self-appraisal: perhaps in the early years of her life she had been able to lay down strong foundations for positive self-esteem.

There would be a long process of personal growth to follow Joan's awakening if her movement towards positive psychological health was to be maintained. In many counselling relationships the counsellor would assist some way along that path, but in our case Joan and the counsellor parted quite early. Near the end of the fourteenth session the counsellor commented on how easily Joan had taken up the restructuring of her life.

She began to cry – a bubbling kind of crying which seemed to represent a mixture of relief and joy. In the review two years later, Joan observed that this was the moment when she knew that she could do the rest herself. She knew that she had rediscovered a happy child who went back beyond her teenage years of abuse and humiliation.

Meeting 15

The ending came quite suddenly. At the beginning of the fifteenth meeting Joan said that she could end very soon, although she would like a little support as she resolved the problem of *'being a new person in an old life'*. This phenomenon is well described in Joan's words:

> I have changed dramatically, and suddenly. I suppose it has been happening for a long time, but it is only now that I'm seeing the full effects of the change. The turn-around is simple to describe – I've started to feel OK about myself. Easy to say, but the consequences are traumatic – it is likely that I am now going to have to quit my husband, restart college, be alone with myself, give up failing at things, be less guarded about expressing my feelings with others and give up manipulating and deceiving people (well, *most* of the time!). The problem is that the whole edifice which is my life is built on these things. It is *all* going to change because I now look on myself differently. *I am a new person in an old life.*

Meetings 16 and 17

These last two meetings were devoted to the following:

1 helping Joan to work out the strategies she would adopt to change those parts of her life which she wanted to change;
2 reviewing the process of their counselling time together; and
3 considering whether there was any 'unfinished business' between them.

During the last two meetings the counsellor felt that he became much more assertive about some of the issues which should be considered, and how that could be done. For instance, he was quite forceful in encouraging Joan to review every area of her life to uncover all the implications occasioned by her change in self-concept. The counsellor also initiated the idea of reviewing the counselling process and the question of unfinished business.

In her exploration of what she might do in the immediate future, Joan paid most attention to the possible ending of her relationship with Roger; the extra voluntary work she would undertake in preparation for her application to a social work degree course; and how she wanted to explore further not just her feelings for her parents, but how they actually had behaved towards her. A fourth issue which Joan introduced took the counsellor completely by surprise, but on reflection made perfect sense. Joan's words describe this best:

> I woke up one morning last week and knew that I now could have children. The realisation took my breath away: I had always seen myself as someone who could never be bothered with children. Now I know that what was behind that was a *fear* of having children – a fear that I was so messed up that I would mess them up. Roger never showed any interest in children either, so that was another way in which we were suited – maybe again that was another reason why I picked him.

A little time was spent outlining the possibility of later 'reviews' and even 'restarts'. And after devoting space to 'reviewing the counselling process', the last main item which the counsellor introduced was the question of whether there was any *unfinished business* between them. For his part he began with a detailed account of his uncertainties and confusion during the beginning of their time together. He had never really explained what had been going on with him at that time, including his difficulties with the other client, Christine, and how these had affected him with Joan. Joan reacted to this information with interest, and told him that it would have been quite helpful to her if he had been more frank at the time and mentioned the other client. She had indeed been very confused by his behaviour: he had seemed 'distracted' and somewhat 'detached' and she had misinterpreted this as a rejection of her. To have had more honest information from the counsellor would have helped.

The only other issue under this heading of 'unfinished business' came from Joan, who admitted that early in their time together she had felt quite a strong sexual attraction towards the counsellor. Her main comment on this was:

> I'm sure this must happen often in this situation. At the beginning of our time together I was extremely vulnerable, and also I was taking a lot of risks. The fact you were showing me a lot of caring was so

unbelievable and exciting. As I grew stronger, that attraction diminished in importance for me, but it is really, really important that you were solid. It feels that that attraction was a really natural thing for me to feel, but if you had responded to it, it would have been terrible – it is really really important that you were solid.

At the very end of the seventeenth and last formal session Joan took the stage for the last time and said:

It is difficult to know what to say, but I want to say something at the end. I find it amazing to see where I am now compared to four months ago. It's almost incomprehensible – I've tried to work out how it happened. It feels complicated – like it feels that *I did it, but that I couldn't have done it without you.* Also, what I treasure is how you were with me. At the times I was most ugly, you moved even closer. And there have been so many times when . . . what we've been doing together has felt like . . . has felt like . . . a kind of loving.

POSTSCRIPT

One month after this last meeting Joan telephoned the counsellor and asked if he would go with her to visit her mother's grave. Joan said that she did not know what she would do there, but that it felt really important for her to go. She did not want to make the visit alone, and would like the counsellor to go with her since she could trust him to cope with whatever happened. The counsellor agreed to this request without difficulty, and the visit took place. During the ten minutes they stood silently at the graveside Joan looked cold and expressionless. However, at the end of this time she screamed and gave her mother's gravestone an almighty kick. She cried a little after that, but seemed more upset by the fact that she had hurt her foot quite badly.

At their review two years later Joan was able to complete this part of her story. For about three months she had continued weekly visits to the graveside on her own. At first she went to the grave to give her hate and then, after talking with an aunt, she went with a tentative understanding of her mother's own vulnerability and finally, on her last visit, she went with forgiveness. Joan never forgave her father, nor did she seek any contact with him.

THE END OF THE COUNSELLING PROCESS

The case-study of Joan and her counsellor illustrates the fact that the end of the counselling process is characterised by *action*. Such action is the outcome of three important developments: the therapeutic movement has occurred which leads to the rapid enhancement of the client's self-acceptance; the various emotional factors preventing a more active life have been reduced; and there is a gradual recognition of a new freedom to make choices and changes which earlier would have seemed impossible. During meetings 11–14 Joan's developing self-acceptance had enabled considerable 'movement': she had re-evaluated her attachment to her husband; understood more about her behaviour towards her bosses; and begun to re-evaluate her abilities and interests. These psychological adjustments enabled Joan to take actions in her life like deciding to resume her studies, beginning to dance again, arranging a holiday with a friend and behaving quite differently in relation to Roger. Instead of being the tormented, conflicted and essentially subservient wife, Joan had quite suddenly been able to withdraw the emotional dependence which she had placed on Roger. She was able to speak and behave more confidently towards him. She could even talk to him about her growing detachment from the relationship, without being paralysed by guilt or fear.

These rapid changes towards the end of the counselling process are quite characteristic of what happens when self-acceptance has been achieved. It is as though the flood-gates which had been holding up the client's personal growth are now open, and all the pressure for change which had been building up over many years surges through and settles quite quickly in its new configuration.

Joan described this phase of the process as one where she was '*a new person in an old life*'. This experience is common for clients who have achieved a turn-around in their self-acceptance. Previously they will have built a life around them which reflected their lack of self-acceptance. They may have been self-defeating, over-submissive and under-valuing of their own abilities. When self-acceptance is achieved all these things can now change, but sometimes at the cost of considerable turmoil. Perhaps the client's relationships at home and at work can be nourished and strengthened by his personal growth but it is possible that these relationships have relied upon the client being weak. Being a new person in an old life can even present a challenge to the client in relation to his children. They will have developed strategies for handling a parent who seemed troubled and conflicted much of the time, and who may have

161

found it difficult to show his love for them. A client who has released himself from the oppression of self-rejection is potentially a much more exciting and loving person to be with, but the client should not be surprised if his children are cautious in their acceptance of this new person whose rapid change they may at first find difficult to trust.

'I never promised you a rose garden' is the title of a famous song and book (Green, 1967). This title is most descriptive of the experience of many clients after successful counselling. While they are pleased with the new self which has emerged, there may also be a tinge of disappointment that their successful progress through counselling does not mean that life is easy thereafter. Sometimes the client has built up a fairy-tale image of what life would be like 'if only I were well'. Such a fairy-tale ending, with its theme of 'living happily ever after', does not bear much resemblance to the reality of having to construct a new life to fit the self which has emerged.

The counsellor can play an important part in helping the client to adjust the lack of fit between his new self and his old life. Joan was able to do much of this for herself, but often the counsellor is an extremely important person for the client at this time. The counsellor may now be the only person in the client's life who understands the change which has taken place and how positively that change is experienced by the client.

In meetings 16 and 17 of our case-study the counsellor also appeared more active in the sense that he initiated activities such as reviewing the process, looking at unfinished business and pressing Joan to consider every detail of her life after the end of counselling. This kind of 'action' on the part of the counsellor can extend to making suggestions on strategies the client might consider, and helping the client to gather information concerning such matters as jobs, legal issues and welfare benefits and resources. This more active role is partly related to the fact that the client is becoming more active, but it also stems from the mutuality which has developed between them. Where mutuality exists the counsellor can trust the client to exert his own power in their relationship. This frees the counsellor to offer information, suggestions and even advice, in the knowledge that the client is not overawed by the counsellor's presence and that he will take what is useful to him and reject what is not. This issue of the fluctuating 'power dynamic' within the therapeutic process is explored in Mearns (1994: 77–9).

ENDINGS WHICH THE COUNSELLOR
REGARDS AS 'PREMATURE'

When a client terminates suddenly without warning or explanation it is appropriate that the counsellor reflects on her own functioning in order to seek understanding, but it is not appropriate for her to assume that the 'fault' must necessarily lie in her. Sometimes the client simply decides that the counselling process is not for him at this time in his life.

Occasionally a client announces his decision to terminate, but stays long enough to explain the reasons. This can give invaluable feedback to the counsellor, who might otherwise only have had fantasies about the client's reasons, but at other times it is more difficult to trust the veracity of the client's statement. For instance, there is what is referred to as the client's *flight into health*. This applies where the client pretends that all his problems have been solved since last week, and no further counselling support is needed! The counsellor should challenge such a statement, but would be wise to do so gently, since the client's trust in her may be low.

Another difficult ending for the counsellor is where the client retains a narrow definition of his problem and judges that the process is finished, either when this is solved or when it becomes obvious that it is not going to be solved quickly. For instance, the client who sees his problem as one of failing to attract women friends may be confused by the counsellor who seeks to help him explore the ways he sees *himself*; or the client who feels 'a bit down' following the death of a close family member may be discouraged when the process appears to take longer than the customary consultation with his doctor. The person-centred counsellor would want to invite the client to explore the wider implications of his presenting problem, but if the client does not acknowledge these, then it is not appropriate for the counsellor to try to enforce her own perception. Clients, after all, have the right to remain at the level of functioning they choose without being coerced by counsellors who are bent on producing fully-functioning persons and nothing less.

PREPARING FOR ENDINGS

As a general rule in person-centred counselling, the client dictates the end-point. If the counselling process has reached the state of mutuality it does not make a great deal of difference whether it is the client or the counsellor who initiates the question of ending, because if the time is not right, the client will feel free to say so. However, mutuality is not always reached in person-centred counselling, but there nevertheless comes a time when it seems to the counsellor that the client may not require their relationship much longer. Perhaps the client has successfully negotiated the main stages of an important life transition, and although the counselling relationship has not developed to the point of mutuality, the client is substantially able to take charge of his life. It is perfectly appropriate in this situation for the counsellor to introduce *tentatively* the question: 'Have you any thoughts on when we should stop?' It is important that the counsellor raises this issue in such a way that the two of them can discuss it openly, without the client feeling that he is *expected* to be ready to stop. Just as it is difficult for the counsellor to appreciate the significance of the therapeutic process for the client, it is not easy for the counsellor to make judgements on how able the client feels to continue on his own. Sometimes a client has made enormous progress in counselling but finds it difficult to imagine how he will continue on his own. 'Ending' for this client may take a little longer while he becomes accustomed to being on his own. Near the end of a lengthy counselling process a client of one of the authors (Mearns) commented: 'Sometimes when I am unsure about something that is happening in my life I sit back and say to myself: "What would I say about this if I was with Dave right now?"' This client was finding a way of becoming her own counsellor and focusing on herself.

From our case-study it appears that Joan first became aware of a natural ending when she realised in meeting 14 that she had rediscovered a happy child who existed before her teenage years of abuse and humiliation. Many changes had happened to her, but this one seemed to carry particular significance. At the beginning of meeting 15 Joan announced that she could end 'very soon'. A useful question to the client at this juncture is what he feels he would want to *do* before the end. In our case-study Joan was clear that she wanted to look at the changes she would make in her life. However, as well as undertaking this task, we find that three other matters were raised by the counsellor. He mentioned the possibility of *reviews* or even *restarts*. It is important to mention these since the client might well assume that counselling is a once-and-for-all offer. Although a major thrust of person-centred counselling is to enable the client to develop the personal strength and self-perception to help him negotiate future difficulties in life, this is not to suggest that he will never again enter into a counselling relationship. On the contrary, if his initial counselling process has been successful it will have equipped him with the ability to use future counselling support efficiently.

The second issue introduced by the counsellor was the idea of *reviewing the counselling process*. One of the benefits of 'reviewing the process' is that it can help both client and counsellor to check their cognitive understanding of the events and process they have been through. Understanding, on a cognitive (thinking) as well as an affective (feeling) level, can also be important for the client as he approaches difficulties in the future; he is able to *think* about his life as well as experience his feelings. However, reviewing the process while it is ending may still not yield complete understanding. The events, the feelings and the relationship may be still too fresh to comprehend fully. Carl Rogers (1961) reports the words of a client who has reached the end of a successful counselling process. Even then, this client cannot fully understand the active ingredients of that process:

> I can't tell just exactly what's happened. It's just that I exposed
> something, shook it up and turned it around; and when I put it back it
> felt better. It's a little frustrating because I'd like to know exactly what's
> going on. (p. 151)

It is interesting that Joan, in our case-study, reflects a similar uncertainty at the very end:

> It's almost incomprehensible. I've tried to work out how it happened. It
> feels complicated – like *I did it, but I couldn't have done it without you.*

It may be that clients, and indeed counsellors, can only understand the therapeutic process fully once they have had some time to be separate from it and to experience its longer-term impact. In compiling the case-study for this book, Joan and the counsellor were able to achieve an understanding of their counselling process which would not have been possible at the point where counselling had ended. Perhaps other clients would value the opportunity to spend some time reviewing their process some two years later.

The third and final element which the counsellor introduced to the ending process was the question of whether they had any *unfinished business* which they might like to complete together. The discipline of asking this question came from the counsellor's other interests in group work, where it is common to create this opportunity at the end of the life of a group.

For the question to be effective it must be asked with plenty of time left, and in such a way that it is regarded as something which is considerably more than a formality. This question is an opportunity for the client to voice questions, uncertainties, or confessions that are usually quite important to him but which would otherwise have gone unsaid. This is the counsellor's last therapeutic intervention, but like all the rest it is not a demand, as evidenced by one client who responded to the question in such a way as to leave the counsellor ever more in mystery: 'unfinished business . . . yes . . . and I think I'm going to keep it that way [*smiles*]!'

AFTER THE END

We have already said that the end need not be final in the sense that the client can arrange reviews or even restarts of the counselling process, but a much more important question is of concern to person-centred practitioners: '*Can clients and counsellors become friends?*' In other counselling approaches which emphasise the power difference between counsellor and client, this question would be a complete non-starter. However, 'boundaries' are in general much less of a problem in person-centred work compared with other counselling approaches because the client is working with a *person* and not just with the *role* of 'counsellor'.

However, even within the person-centred tradition there is a range of opinion on the question of whether clients can become friends. Some person-centred counsellors would assert that 'once a client, always a client'. This is a safe position which preserves integrity, and as such must be respected. However, it does not address the inevitable questions raised by the concept of mutuality. If mutuality is experienced as we have presented it, then the two persons are freely sharing responsibility for the process which takes place between them. Why then are they not free to continue a relationship as friends once the counselling process is ended? In most cases, for the present writers, this question is scarcely contentious: former clients can and do become friends, and even colleagues, in the future.

Underlying our question lurks the much more difficult issue of whether client and counsellor could at any time in the future become sexual partners. This is such an important issue in counselling that we have already devoted some space to it in Chapter 7. In person-centred counselling, as we have described it, the relationship between counsellor and client is one where the counsellor is present as a person and not just as a role. With the development of mutuality this personal relationship is strengthened and becomes more reciprocal. Nevertheless, during the course of counselling we have argued that the nature of the counsellor's responsibility rules out sexual behaviour. We want to go a little further and suggest that even upon completion of counselling the counsellor should for some time thereafter, even perhaps for some years thereafter, consider that the counselling relationship may not be permanently closed and should therefore conform to the usual ethical code as far as sexual behaviour is concerned. The reason for this caution with respect to sexual relations is prompted by three factors. Firstly, we have already noted that, while the state of mutuality is powerful and relatively enduring, it can undergo temporary hiccups and regression. Secondly, neither counsellor nor client can be sure that the ending they mark for the process is indeed final – clients sometimes return to complete a process they had earlier thought was finished. Our third argument for caution relates to the point we made earlier in this chapter concerning the difficulty for the client of understanding fully the counselling process immediately it has ended. We believe that such understanding is a very important ingredient and precedent to relationships which are to change their character so profoundly. The cautious stance we have taken on this issue further reinforces our view that sexual relations in the context of a power difference between the partners represents sexual abuse of a most insidious kind.

Another question which is appropriate for the counsellor after the end of a counselling relationship is '*How have I been affected by this experience?*' We would not expect the counsellor to be so malleable as to be significantly changed by every counselling contact. Equally, the person-centred counsellor who does not change and grow through her experience might question the extent to which she is being fully present in her counselling relationships and wonder about the nature of the climate she is creating for her clients. One of the most important things for person-centred counsellors to appreciate is that in certain respects there is always a danger that they will become *worse* counsellors as they become more experienced. The quality of being fully present in the counselling relationship is enormously difficult to sustain. As the counsellor develops more skills in processes such as empathy, it is easier for her to survive on that and to allow her congruence to suffer to the point where she is less than fully present in the relationship.

In Chapter 3 (Box 3.6) we suggested an exercise which helped the counsellor to focus on her client and the therapeutic relationship. There is perhaps one more focusing question which we might offer to the person-centred counsellor as an aid to monitoring her freshness and commitment.

The question is '*What am I learning from my clients?*' If the person-centred counsellor is still learning from her clients, then the likelihood is that she is being fully present with them. We felt that an appropriate ending to this book would be for the authors to address this fundamental question. Our immediate responses are presented in Box 8.1.

Box 8.1 'What am I Learning from my Clients?'

The authors close the book with their reactions to this question:

DAVE MEARNS: Two things spring immediately to mind. The first is *that I am less clever than I think I am.* My construction of what is happening in counselling for the client often sounds clever and complicated, and then I ask the client, at the very end, what was really important for him, and he says 'because you loved me and I believed you'. I get a frog in my throat and feel pretty stupid.

The second thing that I think of is that *no matter how much experience I get, each new client really is a new beginning.* No matter how much experience I have had with other clients, I have had none with him: I start naked and also a little scared of the unknown.

BRIAN THORNE: My clients are teaching me that I am wiser than I know and that they are, too. They are showing me that when a state of mutuality exists we need have no fear of those times when we seem hopelessly stuck. On the contrary, if we are really committed to staying together in our powerlessness I am discovering that almost always something extraordinary happens. One or other of us has a thought or a feeling or an intuition – and not infrequently we both have it at the same time – and we are stuck no longer. This discovery is the gateway to endless learning and that is why I find it so exciting. What is more, I am discovering that when I can trust my client as much as he or she trusts me, there is every likelihood that we shall experience a sense of interconnectedness which can be transforming for both of us and gives new hope for the future of humankind.

REFERENCES

Axline, V. (1971) *Dibs in Search of Self.* Harmondsworth, Middlesex: Penguin.

Barrett-Lennard, G.T. (1962) 'Dimensions of therapist response as causal factors in therapeutic change', *Psychological Monographs*, 76, No. 43 (Whole No. 562).

Barrett-Lennard, G.T. (1987) *Personal Communication.* Third International Forum on the Person-Centered Approach, La Jolla, California.

Barrett-Lennard, G.T. (1998) *Carl Rogers' Helping System: Journey and Substance.* London: Sage.

Bennis, W. (1986) *Carl Rogers interviewed by Warren Bennis.* Video-tape produced by University Associates Incorporated, San Diego.

Bergin, A.E. and Jasper, L.G. (1969) 'Correlates of empathy in psychotherapy: a replication', *Journal of Abnormal Psychology*, 74: 477–81.

Bergin, A.E. and Solomon, S. (1970) 'Personality and performance correlates of empathic understanding in psychotherapy', pp. 223–36 in J.T. Hart and T.M. Tomlinson (eds), *New Directions in Client-Centered Therapy.* Boston: Houghton-Mifflin.

Bergin, A.E. and Strupp, H.H. (1972) *Changing Frontiers in the Science of Psychotherapy.* Chicago: Aldine-Atherton.

Bettelheim, B. (1987) 'The man who cared for children', *Horizon.* London: BBC Television (video).

Boy, A.V. and Pine, G.J. (1982) *Client-Centered Counseling: a Renewal.* Boston: Allyn & Bacon.

Bozarth, J. (1984) 'Beyond reflection: emergent modes of empathy', pp. 59–75 in R.F. Levant and J.M. Shlien (eds), *Client-Centered Therapy and the Person-Centered Approach*. New York: Praeger.

Bozarth, J. and Temaner Brodley, B. (1986) '*The Core Values and Theory of the Person-Centered Approach*'. Paper prepared for the First Annual Meeting of the Association for the Development of the Person-Centered Approach, Chicago.

Burns, D.D. and Nolen-Hoeksema, S. (1991) 'Coping styles, homework compliance, and the effectiveness of cognitive behavioural therapy', *Journal of Consulting and Clinical Psychology*, 59: 305–11.

Cain, D. (1987) *Personal Communication*. Third International Forum on the Person-Centered Approach, La Jolla, California.

Carkhuff, R.R. (1971) *The Development of Human Resources*. New York: Holt, Rinehart & Winston.

Fiedler, F.E. (1949) 'A comparative investigation of early therapeutic relationships created by experts and non-experts of psychoanalytic, non-directive, and Adlerian schools'. Unpublished doctoral dissertation, Chicago: University of Chicago.

Fiedler, F.E. (1950) 'A comparison of therapeutic relationships in psychoanalytic, non-directive and Adlerian therapy', *Journal of Consulting Psychology*, 14: 436–45.

Gendlin, E.T. (1970) 'A short summary and some long predictions', pp. 544–62 in J. Hart and T. Tomlinson (eds), *New Directions in Client-Centered Therapy*. Boston: Houghton Mifflin.

Gendlin, E.T. (1981) *Focusing*. New York: Bantam.

Gendlin, E.T. (1984) 'The client's client: the edge of awareness', pp. 76–107 in R.F. Levant and J.M. Shlien (eds), *Client-Centered Therapy and the Person-Centered Approach*. New York: Praeger.

Gendlin, E.T. (1996) *Focusing-Oriented Psychotherapy*. New York: Guilford.

Green, H. (1967) *I Never Promised You a Rose Garden*. London: Pan.

Gurman, A.S. (1977) 'The patient's perception of the therapeutic relationship', pp. 503–43 in A.S. Gurman and A.M. Ragin (eds), *Effective Psychotherapy*. New York: Pergamon.

Howe, D. (1993) *On Being a Client*. London: Sage.

Kurtz, R.R. and Grummon, D.L. (1972) 'Different approaches to the measurement of therapist empathy and their relationship to therapy outcomes', *Journal of Consulting and Clinical Psychology*, 39(1): 106–15.

Lafferty, P., Beutler, L.E. and Crago, M. (1991) 'Differences between more and less effective psychotherapists: a study of select therapist variables', *Journal of Consulting and Clinical Psychology*, 59: 305–11.

Lambers, E. (1994a) 'The person-centred perspective on psychopathology:

the neurotic client', pp. 105–9 in D. Mearns, *Developing Person-Centred Counselling*. London: Sage.

Lambers, E. (1994b) 'Personality disorder', pp. 116–20 in D. Mearns, *Developing Person-Centred Counselling*. London: Sage.

Lambers, E. (1994c) 'Borderline personality disorder', pp. 110–13 in D. Mearns, *Developing Person-Centred Counselling*. London: Sage.

Lambers, E. (1994d) 'Psychosis', pp. 113–16 in D. Mearns, *Developing Person-Centred Counselling*. London: Sage.

Levant, R. and Shlien, J. (eds) (1984) *Client-Centered Therapy and the Person-Centered Approach.* New York: Praeger

Lietaer, G. (1984) 'Unconditional positive regard: a controversial basic attitude in client-centered therapy', pp. 41–58 in R. Levant and J. Shlien (eds), *Client-Centered Therapy and the Person-Centered Approach.* New York: Praeger.

Lorr, M. (1965) 'Client perceptions of therapists', *Journal of Consulting Psychology*, 29: 146–9.

Martin, D.G. (1983) *Counseling and Therapy Skills.* Belmont, California: Brooks/Cole.

McDermott, C. (1986) *'Creating the Conditions for Therapy'.* Unpublished paper prepared for the first Facilitator Development Institute (Britain) Therapy Training Course.

Mearns, D. (1985) *'Some Notes on Unconditional Positive Regard'.* Unpublished paper produced for Glasgow Marriage Guidance Service.

Mearns, D. (1986) *'Some Notes on Congruence: Can I Dare to be Me in Response to my Client?'.* Unpublished paper presented to the first Facilitator Development Institute (Britain) Therapy Training Course.

Mearns, D. (1994) *Developing Person-Centred Counselling*. London: Sage.

Mearns, D. (1996) 'Working at relational depth with clients in person-centred therapy', *Counselling*, 7(4): 306–11.

Mearns, D. (1997a) *Person-Centred Counselling Training*. London: Sage.

Mearns, D. (1997b) *The Future of Individual Counselling.* The Ben Hartop Memorial Lecture, 7 May. Published as an Occasional Paper by the University of Durham.

Mearns, D. (1998a) *'Working at relational depth: person-centred intrapsychic "family therapy"'.* Paper presented to the joint conference of the British Association for Counselling and the European Association for Counselling, Southampton, England, 18 September.

Mearns, D. (1998b) 'Managing a primary care service', *The Journal of Counselling in Medical Settings*, 57 (November): 1–5.

Mearns, D. (1998c) 'Person-centred therapy with configurations of self'.

Public Lecture delivered in Athens, Greece, 11 December.

Mearns, D. and Thorne, B. (1988) *Person-Centred Counselling in Action* (First Edition). London: Sage.

Moustakas, C.E. (1959) *Psychotherapy with Children – the Living Relationship.* New York: Harper and Brothers.

Mullen, J. and Abeles, N. (1972) 'Relationship of liking, empathy and therapist's experience to outcome of therapy', pp. 256–60 in *Psychotherapy 1971, an Aldine Annual.* Chicago: Aldine-Atherton.

Neill, A.S. (1960) *Summerhill.* New York: Hart.

O'Leary, C. (1999) *Couple and Family Counselling: A Person-Centred Perspective.* London: Sage.

Orlinsky, D.E., Grawe, K. and Parks, B.K. (1994) 'Process and outcome in psychotherapy – noch einmal', pp. 270–378 in A.E. Bergin and S.L. Garfield (eds), *Handbook of Psychotherapy and Behaviour Change* (Fourth Edition). New York: Wiley.

Patterson, C.H. (1974) *Relationship Counseling and Psychotherapy.* New York: Harper and Row.

Patterson, C.H. (1984) 'Empathy, warmth and genuineness in psychotherapy: a review of reviews', *Psychotherapy,* 21(4): 431–8.

Patterson, C.H. (1985) *The Therapeutic Relationship: Foundations for an Eclectic Psychotherapy.* Monterey: Brooks/Cole.

Purton, A.C. (1998) 'Unconditional positive regard and its spiritual implications', pp. 23–37 in B. Thorne and E. Lambers (eds), *Person-Centred Therapy: a European Perspective.* London: Sage.

Raskin, N. (1974) 'Studies on psychotherapeutic orientation: ideology in practice', *American Academy of Psychotherapists Psychotherapy Research Monographs.* Orlando, Florida: American Academy of Psychotherapists.

Rennie, D.L. (1998) *Person-Centred Counselling: An Experiential Approach.* London: Sage.

Rogers, C.R. (1951) *Client-Centered Therapy: Its Current Practice, Implications and Theory.* Boston: Houghton Mifflin.

Rogers, C.R. (1957) 'The necessary and sufficient conditions of therapeutic personality change', *Journal of Consulting Psychology,* 21(2): 95–103.

Rogers C.R. (1961) *On Becoming a Person.* Boston: Houghton Mifflin.

Rogers C.R. (1963) 'The concept of the fully functioning person', *Psychotherapy: Theory, Research and Practice,* 1(1): 17–26.

Rogers, C.R. (1970). *Encounter Groups.* New York: Harper and Row.

Rogers, C.R. (1974) 'In retrospect: forty-six years', *American Psychologist,* 29(2): 115–23.

Rogers C.R. (1977) *Carl Rogers on Personal Power.* New York: Delacorte.

Rogers, C.R. (1977) *The Right to be Desperate*. Video produced by the American Association for Counseling and Development, Washington D.C.

Rogers C.R. (1979) 'Foundations of the Person-Centered Approach,' *Education*, 100(2): 98–107.

Rogers, C.R. (1980a) *A Way of Being*. Boston: Houghton Mifflin.

Rogers, C.R. (1980b) 'Growing old – or older and growing', *Journal of Humanistic Psychology* 20(4): 15–16.

Rogers, C.R. (1986a) *Freedom to Learn for the '80's.* Colombus, Ohio: Charles E. Merrill.

Rogers, C.R. (1986b) 'A client-centered, person-centered approach to therapy', in L. Kutash and A. Wolf (eds), *A Psychotherapist's Casebook: Therapy and Technique in Practice*. San Francisco: Jossey-Bass.

Rogers, C.R. (1986c) 'A Comment from Carl R. Rogers', *Person-Centered Review*, 1(1): 3–4.

Rogers C.R. (1986d) 'Reflection of feelings', *Person-Centered Review*, 1(4): 375–7.

Rogers C.R., Gendlin, E.T., Kiesler, D.J. and Truax, C.B. (eds) (1967) *The Therapeutic Relationship and its Impact. A Study of Psychotherapy with Schizophrenics*. Madison, Wisconsin: University of Wisconsin Press.

Sachse, R. (1990) 'Concrete interventions are crucial: the influence of the therapist's processing proposals on the client's interpersonal exploration in client-centered therapy', pp. 295–308 in G. Lietaer, J. Rombauts and R. Van Balen (eds), *Client-Centered and Experimental Psychotherapy in the Nineties*. Leuven: Leuven University Press.

Selfridge, F.F. and van der Kolk, C. (1976) 'Correlates of counselor self-actualisation and client-perceived facilitativeness', *Counselor Education and Supervision*, 15(3):189–94.

Slack, S. (1985) 'Reflections on a workshop with Carl Rogers', *Journal of Humanistic Psychology*, 28: 35–42.

Smith, M., Glass, G. and Miller, I. (1980) *The Benefits of Psychotherapy*. Baltimore: Johns Hopkins University Press.

Talmon, M. (1990) *Single Session Therapy*. San Francisco: Jossey-Bass Publishers.

Tausch, R., Bastine. R., Bommert, H., Minsel, W.R. and Nickel, H. (1972) 'Weitere untersuchung der auswirkung und der prozesse klienten-zentrierter gesprächs-psychotherapie', *Zeitschrift für Klinische Psychologie*, 1(3): 232–50.

Tausch, R., Bastine, R., Friese, H. and Sander, K. (1970) 'Variablen und Ergebnisse bei Psychotherapie mit Alternieranden Psychotherapeuten', *Verlag für Psychologie*, 21(1).

Thorne, B. (1985) *The Quality of Tenderness*. Norwich: Norwich Centre Publications.

Thorne, B. (1987) 'Beyond the core conditions', pp. 48–77 in W. Dryden (ed.), *Key Cases in Psychotherapy*. London: Croom Helm.

Thorne, B. (1991a) *Person-Centred Counselling: Therapeutic and Spiritual Dimensions*. London: Whurr Publishers.

Thorne, B. (1991b) *Behold the Man*. London: Darton, Longman and Todd.

Thorne, B. (1992) *Carl Rogers*. London: Sage.

Thorne, B. (1994) 'Developing a spiritual discipline', pp. 44–7 in D. Mearns, *Developing Person-Centred Counselling*. London: Sage.

Thorne, B. (1996) 'The cost of transparency', *Person Centred Practice*, (2): 2–11.

Thorne, B. (1997a) 'Counselling and psychotherapy: the sickness and the prognosis', pp. 153–66 in S. Palmer and V. Varma (eds), *The Future of Counselling and Psychotherapy*. London: Sage.

Thorne, B. (1997b) 'The accountable therapist: standards, experts and poisoning the well', pp. 141–50 in R. House and N. Totton (eds), *Implausible Professions*. Ross-on-Wye: PCCS Books.

Thorne, B. (1997c) 'Spiritual responsibility in a secular profession', pp. 197–213 in I. Horton with V. Varma (eds), *The Needs of Counsellors and Psychotherapists*. London: Sage.

Thorne, B. (1998) *Person-Centred Counselling and Christian Spirituality*. London: Whurr Publishers

Thorne, B. (1999) 'The move towards brief therapy: its dangers and its challenges', *Counselling*, 10(1): 7–11.

Thorne, B. and Lambers, E. (eds) (1998) *Person-Centred Therapy: A European Perspective*. London: Sage.

Truax, C.B. and Carkhuff, R.R. (1967) *Toward Effective Counseling and Psychotherapy*. Chicago: Aldine.

Truax, C.B. and Mitchell, K.M. (1971) 'Research on certain therapist interpersonal skills in relation to process and outcome', pp. 299–344 in A.E. Bergin and S.L. Garfield (eds), *Handbook of Psychotherapy and Behavior Change*. New York: John Wiley.

Vaillant, L.M. (1994) 'The next step in short-term dynamic psychotherapy: a clarification of objectives and techniques in an anxiety-regulating model', *Psychotherapy*, 31: 642–55.

Wexler, D.A. and Rice, L.N. (eds) (1974) *Innovations in Client-Centered Therapy*. New York: John Wiley.

INDEX

175